MW01260007

LITERACY 101

Questions and answers that meet the needs
of real teachers in K-12 classrooms

David Booth

Pembroke Publishers Limited

For Mara and Elijah, who are beginning their literacy lives

© **2016 Pembroke Publishers**
538 Hood Road
Markham, Ontario, Canada L3R 3K9
www.pembrokepublishers.com

Distributed in the U.S. by Stenhouse Publishers
480 Congress Street
Portland, ME 04101
www.stenhouse.com

All rights reserved.
No part of this publication may be reproduced in any form or by any means electronic or mechanical, including photocopy, scanning, recording, or any information, storage or retrieval system, without permission in writing from the publisher. Excerpts from this publication may be reproduced under licence from Access Copyright, or with the express written permission of Pembroke Publishers Limited, or as permitted by law.

Every effort has been made to contact copyright holders for permission to reproduce borrowed material. The publishers apologize for any such omissions and will be pleased to rectify them in subsequent reprints of the book.

Funded by the Government of Canada
Financé par le gouvernement du Canada | Canadä

Ontario
Ontario Media Development Corporation
Société de développement de l'industrie des médias de l'Ontario

---

Library and Archives Canada Cataloguing in Publication

Booth, David W. (David Wallace), author
    Literacy 101 : questions and answers that meet the needs of real teachers / David Booth.

Issued in print and electronic formats.
ISBN 978-1-55138-315-6 (paperback).--ISBN 978-1-55138-916-5 (pdf)

    1. Literacy--Study and teaching. I. Title.

LC149.B65 2016   302.2'244   C2016-903248-5
                                           C2016-903249-3

Editor: David E. Kilgour
Cover Design: John Zehethofer
Typesetting: Jay Tee Graphics Ltd.

Printed and bound in Canada
9 8 7 6 5 4 3 2 1

MIX
Paper from
responsible sources
FSC
www.fsc.org   FSC® C004071

Contents

Foreword

How do we help teachers — both novice and experienced — deepen their understanding of best literacy practices? How might teachers' assumptions about significant literacy techniques be clarified, validated, and stretched in order to provide success for all student learners? How can the literacy agenda in a teacher education program best guide teachers into the theory and practice of effective reading, writing, media, technology, and talk?

Like other teacher professionals, I have many questions about these issues. But growing as a teacher necessitates that I seek out the questions filtering through the minds of my students. For the past twenty years, I have been an instructor in the teacher education program at the Ontario Institute for Studies in Education, and each year I recognize the challenge of collaborating with students to discover best practices for teaching literacy. On the first day of my literacy course I encourage students to work towards a definition of literacy instruction, and this definition will likely evolve as the year unfolds. I explain that they will have (and should have) many questions that will lead them to discover and learn. In the final class, I invite students to create a list of core questions about literacy — assessment, technology, integration, differentiation, text choices, timetabling, spelling, etc. — after having been in the program for ten months. What are their focus questions now that they are about to teach literacy? I have shared these questions with David Booth, my friend and colleague, who has used them as a structure for presenting the insights, opinions, anecdotes, and theoretical underpinnings that have emerged from his teaching and research over many years.

Literacy 101 is an overview of where we are now as literacy educators, and where we can continue to develop and change as classroom practitioners. David knows that answers to complex questions need to be in a state of flux, ready for new directions, new conceptualizing, but as a frame for where we should be at this time in our educational knowledge, this book indeed represents a solid and practical course in teaching literacy.

Larry Swartz
Toronto, June 2016

Introduction

Blessed is the one who readeth...

Revelation 1:3

Watching my young grandchildren as they join the literacy club has caused me to reassess my thoughts on how we help our students grow in their reading, writing, and proficiency with technology. I've had to take stock of where I am in my professional and personal life right now, in this space and time. I teach a course in literacy to teachers taking graduate degrees, and each year I wade through the journal articles, the new books, and the websites, I attend the major conferences on literacy and language arts, I talk to my colleagues at my university and other schools, and I visit and work with teachers in their classrooms on issues of practice. And still I have questions about how we can best support our students in developing their meaning-making processes with the texts they meet, inside and outside school. But this makes sense when you "read" the continually changing world in which children, including my grandkids, will find themselves, and how we as teachers will have to respond in order to adapt our pedagogy and practice to their needs and wishes.

I began my career in the fall of 1958 teaching forty-two grade-five students at a school in Hamilton, Ontario. The principal helped me establish a timetable, and reading was to happen each day from 11:00 until noon, after a spelling time from 10:30 until 11:00. Each week there would be one writing period, called "creative writing." On Friday afternoons, all the students would gather in the gym from 3:00 to 4:00 to watch a film. That comprised the literacy component of my life as a teacher.

During the second week of term, a reading consultant arrived at my door with forty-five books. There were fifteen copies each of three titles: *Young Canada Reads* for the "low" group, *Gay Adventurers* for the middle group, and *Proud Processions* for the gifted. I was to be the pilot teacher for a project called Three Group Reading. The students would be divided into three groups by ability; there were enough of the three different texts for fifteen students in each group, but the manuals had not arrived (nor did they ever). I was instructed to write twelve questions on the board for each group to answer. This would keep them occupied as I brought one group at a time to sit on the floor at the front; the students would then take turns reading the selections aloud, one by one. Later, I was to mark all of their answers in their notebooks.

I was a totally ineffective reading teacher. The students droned on reading aloud one after the other, we never explored any strategies for improvement, and their answers were marked in their notebooks and never discussed. I would have continued this way, I suppose, for years, except for classroom visits by the English supervisor for Hamilton schools, William H. Moore, who opened for me the world of literacy and literature. He demonstrated and shared such wonderful classroom practices as reading aloud engaging novels to the class, reading powerful poems aloud with the students, using the public library as a resource for bringing personal choice to the students' reading, having students write poems and stories from their life experiences, incorporating small group discussions within every lesson, buying dictionaries and thesauruses for students to use when they wanted them, and most important, he taught us all to use dramatization and role-playing as responses to the texts we were reading. The students became what they had read, through drama activities, and I found a way to be inside my own teaching and alongside my students.

All these strategies became part of mainstream language arts and English teaching over the next decades. Bill Moore's teachings were supported and strengthened by the dozens, if not hundreds, of research projects carried out by educators in government, universities, and school districts, and interpreted by excellent teachers who began writing books for teachers about their classroom practice, backed by the strong research now available.

Patricia Alexander and Emily Fox, in their article "A Historical Perspective on Reading Research and Practice, Redux," offer us a historical and critical review of the different perspectives and lenses that frame the different issues and concerns of educators in how to research and teach the process of reading. In great detail and with scholarly insights, they cover the theoretical conceptions about the learner and the learning process that directed policies in teacher preparation and government curricula over the last sixty years. Their work helps us to recognize the changes in the research and the teaching of reading and writing that had such an impact on how we educated new teachers, and how we offered professional development for practicing teachers. We now have to add to this discussion the effects of technology in the classroom and in the out-of-school lives of the students. This overwhelming factor in communication modalities means we need to be aware of the new media and the messaging affected by them.

As school districts require research-based and data-driven learning/teaching events, we will need educators to find ways of interpreting these studies for classroom practice. I have many heroes who have provided me with research in literacy over the decades, too many to list, and throughout this book I will include supportive texts for teachers in the margins next to the issues under consideration.

I have tried to share my understanding of the current teachings in literacy and their implications for how children become readers and writers of different types of texts. The queries I received from Larry Swartz's teacher candidates, as detailed in his foreword, forced me to re-think and re-search what we now consider effective processes and strategies in the new frames for literacy. Using these core questions has given me a structure for collecting my thoughts on many of the present issues concerning literacy learning and teaching, and I hope they will provide an overview of where we are in our research and practice.

These are the questions of teachers who want to continue to grow as professionals, and my thoughts about those queries, from my computer to your challenges. A teacher I met at a conference in New York came up to me at the close of my talk and, with tears in her eyes, asked me, "How do you get to be a good teacher?" Spontaneously I replied, "By hanging around good teachers." And I have referred in this book to many readings of and conversations with good educators that have helped me in my reflections, and I hope that my responses to students' questions will lead to more questions that may help us move closer to maximizing how students learn about and through literacy, and how we can best support them on their journeys.

David Booth
Toronto, June 2016

We cannot know through language what we cannot imagine...
Those who cannot imagine cannot read.

Elliot Eisner, *The Arts and the Creation of Mind*

WORDS MATTER...

words we hear
words we read
words we know
words we chant
words we sing
words we recognize
words we read aloud
words that make us laugh
words we take apart
words we solve
words we construct
words with patterns
words we string together
words that tell stories
words that share information
words that puzzle us
words we love
words we write
words that have families
words from our elders
and
words we are given as gifts

1

Why is "literacy" such a popular term in teaching today?

What does "literacy education" mean for us as teachers?

Literacy was once defined simply as the ability to read and write. Today we understand that there are multiple literacies: we recognize the variety of ways to make shared meaning in our lives — language, of course (both oral and written), music, art, graphics, technology, dance, and, in fact, all the symbol systems. For young people today, learning will require opportunities to explore meaning-making with many of these forms, and in new combinations of them, such as the visual text literacies found in their electronic, computer-filled world. There is not one definition of literacy since literacy practices are multiple and shift based on the context, speaker, text, or the function of the literacy event (e.g., performing a Google search vs. reading a historical novel).

Even our definition of the term "text" now extends beyond the traditional printed or written work using an alphabetic code or symbol system. Now "text" can be any message intended to communicate through a variety of modes: written, visual, tactile, oral (e.g., an audio book), a magazine, a painting, a film, a computer screen, narrative, information, list, opinion, persuasive editorial, poetry, song, script, instruction and procedural, graphics, and more. In this book I will be using the term "text" in its widest sense. I do, however, stress printed texts, online and on the page, because the ability to work with the printed code is still a prerequisite for literacy in most of its forms.

As teachers, we must learn to negotiate the varied terrain of literacy, recognizing that every student has a right to read and write what he or she wants to read and write at some time during the day, but, as wise parents and teachers know, we also require the strength to ensure that students experience text forms that can change their lives in different ways, texts that make them laugh and cry, novels and films that portray lives so like or unlike their own, information about science and geography and people and health that move them further into ideas and issues.

That is why school can be such a powerful force in teaching literacy: it provides a built-in community for exploring our text-generated ideas. We bring our own life needs to every experience with text. When we explore a text we have met, when we respond to it through discussion, writing, research, role-playing, or art, we add to our own understanding, we alter our perspectives, we create a new text that lives alongside the original, adding to our grasp of the subjects and issues we have begun to explore. We change ourselves as we re-think, re-tell, or re-imagine the original text. We re-read, re-view, re-listen, and we find the text has become a whole new experience.

What follows are four different approaches to the meaning of literacy education. Feel free to choose or focus on those that speak to you:

THE RESEARCHER

Here is how one research team has categorized the different abilities required for literacy:

- *to break the code of texts:* recognizing and using the fundamental features and architecture of written texts, including alphabet, sounds in words, spelling, conventions, and patterns of sentence structure and text;
- *to participate in the meanings of text:* understanding and composing meaningful written, visual, and spoken texts from within the meaning systems of particular cultures, institutions, families, communities, nation-states, and so forth;
- *to use texts functionally:* traversing the social relations around texts; knowing about and acting on the different cultural and social functions that various texts perform both inside and outside school and knowing that these functions shape the way texts are structured, their tone, their degree of formality, and their sequence of components;
- *to critically analyze and transform texts:* understanding and acting on the knowledge that texts are not neutral, that they represent particular views and silence other points of view, influence people's ideas; and that their designs and discourses can be critiqued and redesigned, in novel and hybrid ways.

Allan Luke and Peter Freebody,
"A Map of Possible Practices"

THE CHILDREN'S BOOK AUTHOR

Well-known children's author and educator Mem Fox describes three "secrets" of reading and says that good readers learn to use these three secrets "simultaneously, rapidly and efficiently":

- understanding the world (general knowledge, conversations, life experiences);
- knowing how language works in different forms and media (speech, poetry, books, the Internet, newspapers, advertisements, etc.)
- seeing how print works (letters, meanings, upper and lower case, punctuation, etc.).

THE EDUCATOR

Education is a process of working to master or acquire different discourses at increasing levels of complexity, and that full literacy implies an ability to work with all kinds of texts, especially those that seem unfamiliar. To be open to what a text offers depends on the action of the imagination.

Karen Gallas, *Imagination and Literacy*

MY APPROACH

For me, literacy education is about enabling the reader/viewer/listener
- to make the most meaning possible
- with this specific text form
- at this particular time and
- in this particular context.

As a child, I read the novel *Black Beauty* and was captivated by the adventure of two horses within the British context of its time. As a teacher, I began to examine the social issues reflected in the book and noticed the literary conceit of the talking horses with dialects indicating social class. As a literacy educator, I am aware of its specific place as a classic, of its limited appeal to contemporary readers, and the need to examine the cultural context and the language with children. And then, of course, there are the films, made in 1946 and 1994 — different texts altogether. All of these versions and insights came at different times and in different contexts in my life, as a reader, a father, a teacher, and a lecturer. Making meaning is a lifelong process, constantly transforming as experience and context change.

What are the new literacies?

Jane Baskwill's *Attention-Grabbing Tools for Involving Parents in their Children's Learning* reminds us to work collaboratively with parents and caregivers in bringing literacy for life to our students.

The so-called new literacies are profoundly shaping the ways in which we view and use language. Just as the telephone altered communication strategies, our students will encounter a wide and perhaps unthought-of variety of information and communication technologies. Just think of video cameras, web editor programs, spreadsheets, listservs, blogs, Power Point, virtual worlds, avatars, and more. Our traditional way of thinking about and defining literacy will be insufficient if we hope to provide youngsters with what they will need to be full participants in the world of the future. Our youngsters will require technological expertise in their home, work, and civic lives. They will need to be plugged in (or wireless) for survival.

Social media require an approach to literacy that, as New Literacies authority Gunther Kress writes in "Design and Transformation: New Theories of Meaning," "attempts to capture and recognize the multiple forms, multiple sites and multiple purposes of communication, to show them in their social/cultural environment."

For me, the following points highlight some of the most important and exciting features of the new literacies movement:
- the development of the social self and identity as a factor in engaging with texts and responses;
- the importance of parents and family culture in literacy development;
- the enhancement of connections between "outside" and "inside" school;
- "frontloading" to support comprehension before introducing a text;
- shifting the balance of power in the roles of teacher and student to facilitate identity development;

Jennifer Rowsell is an authority on the new literacies, and in her book *Working with Multimodality* she gives examples of classrooms exploring interconnecting modes of texts.

- increasing the awareness of and respect for diversity to fight stereotyping and prejudice.

Can I teach comprehension or is it just a memory test?

It depends on which text, and which context. Some worlds are easy for us to enter: we have seen that mountain; we have lived in that city; we have walked past those bulrushes; we have owned a dog like the one in the book. Others are more difficult: we need the deft author or artist who invites us in, the clever storyteller who draws us along, or the perceptive teacher who builds with us a suitable context. And the landscape of our minds is constantly shifting as we experience a text, when we reflect, when we engage with other texts, and when we consider the ideas and opinions of others. Our comprehension alters as our life goes on, and our response to a text is never frozen.

Comprehension — or meaning-making, or understanding, or interpretation — involves using information from the text (words, sounds, and/or images) along with the knowledge and previous experiences in the mind and heart of the reader/viewer/listener. We know that reading printed text is more than pronouncing words. It is more than attempting to second-guess the intent of the author. Reading is a process of interpretation and negotiation from our lived and vicarious experiences at a moment in time. We need to help students constantly expand their abilities to process print, from a single word on a billboard to a dense novel translated from Russian. From our first beginning steps in reading, texts continue to present challenges to us for the rest of our reading lives — the words and language patterns, the structure and organization of different kinds of texts, our purpose in reading or viewing a particular text, and especially the content and our connections to it. Comprehension, then, is the process of constructing personal meaning as I, the reader, focus on a particular text, make sense of the author's reason for writing and my reason for reading, interpret the language and style, the information and ideas, and somehow synthesize the whole experience and integrate it into my own present culture of understanding.

In reality, we don't work through literal levels, then move to inferential predictions, and conclude with critical generalizations. Instead, we work in a nonlinear fashion, changing our judgments as we glean information and discover implications, anticipating and adjusting predictions as the context deepens. All these processes are components of higher-order thinking, the guesswork that leads to broadened consciousness. We need to design classroom activities that will provide opportunities for using various thinking processes when young people engage with different text forms.

Years ago, American author and illustrator Charles Reasoner taught me to help readers to *reveal their comprehension*, and that turned me around. He answers the question about how we teach comprehension: we assist a child in growing as a reader, as he/she reveals thoughts and feelings about a reading selection: we try to enrich and extend the reader's perceptions and perspectives about the text, deepening an understanding of how the writer and the reader make meaning together. The reader questions the text, explores puzzlements, debates issues, rethinks original perceptions through interactive conversations, sometimes with a group, at other times in a notebook, and at times through interpreting thoughts with art or poetry. We help the reader to notice style and language, to become aware of how the particular genre functions. Comprehension, then, is assembled like Lego blocks: readers are part of the process of comprehending a text. They matter; the text matters; why they are reading matters; everything matters. We aren't what we read; we read what we are, and what we can become.

Why do some students not understand a text while others "get it"?

Over the years, I have come to realize the complexity of comprehending a text that we may encounter. But comprehension is not just a score on a test featuring one type of text; understanding and sense-making depend on so many bits and pieces in our experience with a particular text at a particular time. I have difficulty with many types of text, from tax forms to manuals to political biographies, depending on my time, my background, my needs, my work, and a dozen other factors. The following points may clarify our understanding of what it may mean to "comprehend" a text for a student at this phase in his/her life. As you read through the prompts, you are finding ways of developing a picture of the child's reading processing, alongside your strategies for assessing progress

Does the student:
- have an interest in and/or an appreciation of the text?
- make connections to the text from both life and literacy experiences?
- show familiarity with the ideas presented in the text?
- demonstrate an awareness of the characteristics of the genre (e.g., report, novel, poem)?
- experience feelings of success and competence as a reader?
- have an understanding of the goal for reading a particular text selection?
- take responsibility for choosing the text to be read?
- respond to the text through discussion, writing, etc.?
- accept the attributes, opinions, and behaviours of peers during reading activities?
- participate in a public shared experience, a performance, or a test?

With the following checklist, you can observe, interact, question and notice behaviours and responses that can direct your own attempts at promoting a better understanding of the text's effects on the reader's comprehension, from building background to supporting the reader during the time he/she is reading, and after reading the text for reflection and rethinking.

Does the teacher:
- carefully select the material for interest and ability?
- offer pre-text support setting the stage for reading?
- give the student a sense of ownership of the reading experience?
- engage the reader in the reading activity?
- support intensive and extensive reading?
- regularly monitor the young reader in order to give help when it's needed?
- offer prompts as strategies used to support the reader while reading the text?
- support independent reading (e.g., with a tape of the book)?
- develop a mentoring relationship with the young reader (e.g., as facilitator, mentor, tester)?

- create follow-up activities that promote reflections, rereading, or revisiting of the text?

What is the place of technology and the computer in my literacy program?

An exciting new book by Clare Kosnik and colleagues, *Building Bridges: Rethinking Literacy Teacher Education in a Digital Era*, outlines the connections between our literacy teaching and the impact of technology on classroom dynamics.

At the end of a teaching session concerning literacy, feeling pleased with myself, I was asked by a boy if I had heard of the woman who lived in a tree. When I said I had not, he told us a bit about her, and then suggested that he would get some information together and courier it to me. He was eight years old. Three days later, a package did indeed arrive at my desk, containing a complete dossier of printouts of articles and photographs about this woman, along with a table of contents, a summary the boy had written from the printouts, his reflections on the subject, and a collage he had made from the colour photos he had downloaded from different websites. Welcome to the world of digital information.

Everyone I know working in the area of education and literacy spends hours each day reading and writing, constructing and viewing, on some type of keyboard, staring at a screen. The digital world is everywhere, and I am now a citizen. The disparities between the plugged-in or wireless electronic home and the traditional school contribute to the alienation many students feel about what goes on in their classroom. How can we build on their digital literacies as we re-conceptualize how we could teach reading and writing?

Some schools have one computer at the back of the classroom; others have a computer lab along the hallway; others have a trained librarian with print and computer resources to assist the teacher; others have a portable computer for each student and a SMART Board for the teacher. I am so impressed with the ways in which schools have organized to give their students opportunities to become computer-literate, but more importantly to use technology to support and enhance their own learning events. But I remember my son's kindergarten class; there was one computer in the corner, and his excellent teacher gave each five-year-old a chance to work with it once a week. That was thirty years ago, but there are still inequities in our students' technological education depending on funding and location

Schools have made great progress in making technology available to all their students, from technical labs and moveable carts of computers to iPads for every student to students' own hand-held devices. Technology in literacy education needs to be the "new normal."

Hella Richter-Glinos writes:

> My teaching assignment this year — Genius Hour on rotary. Every class in our school, from kindergarten to grade 5, has one period per week, during which they come to the Genius Hour lab to use technology to complete inquiry passion projects. Our Genius Hour Program is all about helping students to develop literacy and inquiry skills by tapping into their interests. Our students love seeing their ideas in print. We use speech-to-text technology so that even students with learning exceptionalities, that affect their writing, can be successful authors.

Students today think of themselves as programmers and as interface designers when they read and generate texts on a computer. They interweave such modes as written text, sounds, animation, and video to enhance their assignments. Computers can also be used to visualize abstract concepts or to solve problems. As a result, we can no longer view the texts we use during literacy teaching as primarily written or linguistic: they are made up of images, of sounds, of movement, just as the texts that students read and enjoy at home are both print and electronic. Technology is part of a larger set of social relationships. The technology of the future will bring an ever-increasing flow of visual information, which students will need to learn to comprehend, analyze, and apply to new situations. We need to help students be active and critical in their use of multimedia, and vigilant so that they do not get lost in cyberspace.

Corey Follett's grade-seven students examined the past and present roles of girls in Afghanistan. The students were divided into action research groups, each with different areas to discover (education, family roles, well-being, etc.), and used the Internet as a research database. They compared their findings, noted sources, considered the reliability and credibility of the data, compiled summaries, and interviewed a military soldier who had been stationed in Afghanistan for two tours.

These students were learning how to research, how to question sources, how to read the lines and in between the lines, and how to use the Internet with critical eyes. Technology was a valuable tool, and they were learning the craft.

Why do we blog?

The philosophy of "schools without walls" is best understood with the use of technology that allows students to travel the globe at will. There are now safeguards that can be implemented for school use that still permit access to many excellent sites. Blogging, or web logging, can give students a forum for virtual conversations with classmates and the teacher, and connect them to other voices in different locales. Caleigh Dunfield writes about her classroom blog from a school in New Brunswick:

> Initially, I hoped to create a simple site with the primary function being a common place to connect with my students and their parents. But it was when the site began to connect students with each other, with peers in other grades, and eventually with an extended online community that I realized its true value as a tool to support and enrich student learning. Our class website afforded us the opportunity to reach out into the community, whether locally or well beyond our small-town doorstep. For example, one of my students received a comment on his review of a graphic novel from someone in San Francisco; another two boys received so much positive feedback for what can best be described as their "Ode to Country Livin'" that one wrote "I LOVE POETRY!!!" in his agenda, prompting my heart to skip a beat.

Royan Lee, blogger and teacher, explains his rationale for classroom blogging:

> Blogging, when used as a digital portfolio and network of thinking, is an immensely powerful tool. In our class, students use blogs to read, write, reflect, create, share, mentor, lead, and learn how to be a contemporary networked learner. They post assignments, reading responses, video, audio, slideshows, formal pieces of writing, informal and spontaneous thoughts, drawings, poetry, and even music.

You can read a full description of Caleigh Dunfield's classroom program in my book *Exploding the Reading*.

I assign my students blogging tasks and open-ended, what-have-you-got-to-say tasks that encourage divergence of thought. In the former, one of "Mr. Lee's Posts" might be a reading response question, writing prompt, or a thinking challenge. In the latter, the students' "Personal Posts" encourage free form thoughts and opinions. They are either sharing a reflection on a text I have assigned or making a comment about life in general.

If you were to ask which one of these results in the most spectacular thought and work, what would I say? The Personal Posts in a landslide. My students are reading a diverse array of text genres and forms; in addition, they are writing or creating texts using paragraph writing, storyboarding for digital comics (Bitstrips) and multimedia slideshows (Animoto), visual art (iPad, Glogster), voice (podcasting), presentation tools (Prezi), and so on. In other words, they get to dabble a lot in different media of communication, as well as hone and craft their favorites and strengths. It's amazing to see what students will do if you let them flourish in the forms of communication they are really passionate about.

Here is the rationale Royan developed with his class for this high-yield avenue for thought expression and connection.
Blogging:
- provides a real audience for our work;
- serves as a portfolio for our work and thinking;
- allows us to see each other's work and provide feedback on it;
- lets us practice how to post online and how to craft our digital footprint;
- gives us teacher support and guidance on how to use the social media we are already using on our own;
- teaches us to think critically about our online presence, and the importance of creating a positive one;
- creates a community of learners;
- lets us practice contemporary literacy skills;
- lets us stay connected even away from class time;
- makes all the kids feel they are in one big class;
- means handwriting has nothing to do with the quality of your work;
- is really fun.

I first met Royan Lee in his middle school, and asked him to share his ideas on using technology throughout the day in my book *Caught in the Middle*. He has continued to develop his expertise as a technology wizard with students and teachers.

Is technology replacing books?

Yes and no. Technology is certainly a force to be reckoned with. While working in a pilot program with researcher Tina Benevides, in an all-boys grade seven class, I wanted to explore research strategies using the Internet with a class set of iPads. I asked the boys to find information on the Internet about a hero who interested them. I then wrote their responses on the SMART Board. Their heroes ranged from Batman to Terry Fox to J.F.K. As the list grew longer, I asked the boys to classify their responses, and they came up with these categories: political heroes, celebrities, artists, sports heroes, war heroes, people who demonstrated courage, and when one boy shouted out "Jesus!" we added religious heroes. The lists they had discovered on the Internet could not have been found in any one reference book.

As they dug deeper into what defines a hero, a student called out, "Nellie McClung." I asked him to tell us why she should be included, and he read out information about her in a halting voice. Then he shared other names from his list, suddenly stating, "Dr. Booth, these are all women, and they're Canadian." This was the same lad who had some difficulty reading the story the rest of us had read. His discovery represented for me the value of this kind of freewheeling research. It's the contemporary digital equivalent of what I used to do physically years ago: instead of searching in the card catalogue, I would wander in the stacks of books, backpacking in "idea countries" and surprising myself into new discoveries.

These boys had stumbled upon Greek myths, athletes who had passed on, comic heroes, lawmakers, and ordinary folk who had behaved in extraordinary ways. They tried dozens of websites, used hundreds of cue words, and argued and debated the qualities of heroic action. Then the moment arrived that we as teachers hope for in every teaching situation: a student asked whether Leonardo da Vinci could be classified as a hero. There were comments back and forth, until one boy informed us that the artist had painted the Mona Lisa, and that alone should classify him as a hero. There was consensus, and we added him to the list. I asked the class to find a picture of the painting on their iPads, and in a classroom in Northern Ontario, far from the Louvre in Paris, twenty-two boys held up images of the Mona Lisa. I felt that I was in a Fellini film. When one student said, "I heard that there is a secret code in her left eyebrow," twenty-two left eyebrows appeared in close-up on their screens, and a new inquiry was born.

It can't be either/or. We can be plugged in at times, and still gather together and sit in a circle, to listen to a tale two thousand years old. Yet computer use can include programs involving print resources that connect the students to the worlds they inhabit, while at the same time stretching their abilities and interests. We can include novels, biographies, poems, columns, and articles online and on the page that represent the best writers and artists we can find who will enrich the lives of our students. Resources that touch the emotions and the intellect have a much greater opportunity for moving readers into deeper frames of understanding.

We have all witnessed the enthusiasm with which students embrace technology. Information technologies can free students from physical constraints, motivate them, allow them, no matter where they live, to connect with others around the world, provide them with purpose for their projects, and give them access to powerful problem-solving tools. From the simplest talking CD that allows a non-reader to enjoy a story, to the hypermedia software that gives students the power to create their own multimedia presentations, technology is a tool that can empower our students. I bought my grandkids (five and seven years old) a small laptop computer for Christmas last year — along with two books each.

Michael Fullan's book *Stratosphere: Integrating Technology, Pedagogy, and Change Knowledge* contains his current observations on the changes technology is bringing to schools, and he includes our project with boys and iPads.

What is critical literacy? Does it apply to every kind of text?

With the increasing complexity of the texts in our lives, students need to move beyond literal understanding, and to think deeply and critically about what texts say and mean. Since the texts were created by individuals and groups who have been influenced by their own contexts in society — the choices, the values, and the authority they assume — students can learn to explore their own meanings with a particular text, form their viewpoints from their own developing lives. Who they are at a particular stage in life will determine to a great extent how they interact with a particular text.

Consider the importance of critical literacy on the Internet. Students are surfing the web and constructing their own individualized texts, evaluating sites, processing information, and interpreting data, so that they can connect themselves to the world. Critical literacy is now being seen as a mainstream strategy. We want to encourage students to become more critical in their use of all media, including the Internet; we need to teach them to be active and critical readers who can make the most connections possible.

I was invited to read to a combined grade-seven-and-eight class of sixty students in an area of southwestern Ontario surrounded by tomato farms. I wanted a strong story that would engage the students, since I was a stranger to them and would need to hold their attention. I began with Eve Bunting's book *Smoky Night*, illustrated by David Diaz.

Bunting's stories work on many levels, and I wanted these youngsters to see beyond the words and images, with a critical lens. This intense story examines urban violence, inspired by the Los Angeles riots. Yet Bunting subtly embeds issues of racism inside the story of two families and their two cats who have to flee the burning of their apartments. Because of the details in the illustrations, the reader's assumptions about race are challenged, and the social needs of the families are revealed.

The students' puzzlements from the story determined the directions of our discussions: their first concern was the issue of riots. Living near Detroit, they had heard family anecdotes about the riots of 1967, and wanted to understand the reasons why citizens decide to cause such destruction in their own community.

The conversation went on for some time, with bits of information being fed in, and many opinions and more questions. The students said they would research the incidents online and continue the discussion later. But one girl shared a closing comment: "I think a riot begins like a huge, painful boil on the surface of the city; eventually, it just bursts." That showed critical thinking, an interpretation and extension of what was in the original text.

Students are constantly exposed to a wide variety of texts, both in and out of school. As they encounter this array of texts, critical literacy becomes a tool for helping them interpret the messages that are embedded in them, connecting them to their present understanding of what they know, or what they thought they knew, and moving them into unfamiliar territory. Critical literacy encourages them to question the authority of texts and address issues of bias, perspective, and social justice that they may contain. Many readers assume that print materials are automatically true.

I find prompts like the following useful to keep in mind when cultivating critical literacy:

- What is the author's background and experience?
- Whose point of view is expressed?
- Is the information accurate and believable?
- What does the author, filmmaker, or artist want you to think?
- Whose voices are missing, silenced, or discounted?
- Which characters in the text seem to hold all the power?
- Were characters or events portrayed in ways that were unexpected?
- Do you belong to any of the groups in this text?
- Which is the world like to the people in this text?
- Were things left out of the illustrations that you thought needed to be included?

- How might alternative perspectives or viewpoints be represented?
- What might you add to the story to make it more complete?
- Can you research the author and his or her perspective?
- What do other sources of information say about these events, characters, and issues?
- What action might you take from what you have learned?

What kinds of texts should students read/view/listen to/engage with?

A teacher in her first teaching position told me that she arrived to find there were no books on the few shelves in her classroom. Thus her job as a literacy mentor began. We know that we need to incorporate satisfying, supportive, and enriching materials of all kinds in our classrooms, continually building print and technology resources that enable students to grow and stretch as young readers, writers, and researchers, helping them to recognize the personal power that literacy success can provide. We are fortunate if we have a school library to help us.

We can classify texts by genre, but we have two ways of describing that term: 1) by form (e.g., novels, scripts, poems), and 2) by function (e.g., persuasion, argument, explanation). Elementary schools have moved into teaching genre by function, and some schools spend months on one genre form, such as reading and writing opinions. For me, genre definitions are always cloudy, since a poem can be a procedural piece of writing, a narrative, an argument, and so on. Novels can be written in free verse, as a diary, or as a series of letters. That is why I like thinking of genre as determined by the author's intent. If Beverly Cleary feels that *Love That Dog* is a novel, written with small chunks of poetic texts, then that works for me. If *Dear Mr. Henshaw* is written as a series of letters but looks like a novel, that is what I will call it. The more familiar students are with the characteristics of a text, the more accessible it will become, and the more easily they will be able to read it. They will know what to expect when they read a novel, a science text, a poem, or a letter; they will recognize the intent of a speech, an editorial, or an article.

Think of all the diverse and language-rich resources we could find to fill our classrooms: some we can use as read-aloud material; some will open other worlds of information and research; some will work well for demonstrating a particular point; some will be part of the language play that brightens our community time; some will be effective as the shared text for our small-group time; some will support independent reading; some will act as mentor texts, working with the style, the structure, or the format, models for the students' own writing; and some will be there just to strengthen our own resolve as literacy teachers.

The following is a list of different genres that should be part of any literacy program if at all possible given the limits of budgets and availability:
- novels — contemporary and classic, and now graphic — at different reading levels, added to throughout the year, online and in print;
- nonfiction in books, articles, and websites;
- publishers' anthologies — full of useful short selections, often leveled, for working with small groups;
- picture books that offer students in all grades an aesthetic experience with words and visuals;

- magazines, both to be read and to be used as art resources for responding and creating;
- taped versions of books of all kinds, for both struggling and gifted readers;
- interactive computer software and the Internet;
- poetry anthologies to be read and to be listened to, including poems that would be undiscovered unless we introduced them;
- letters, memos, YouTube films, and advertisements to use in our demonstrations;
- student writing that highlights the writer's craft or that represents emotional power;
- teacher writing that illustrates who we are as learners;
- bits and pieces saved from the texts of our lives that we need to share with our students;
- songs to read aloud as we sing the lyrics together;
- book talks, discussions, guest speakers, video clips — voices from outside the walls yet resonating within;
- jokes, riddles, puns, funny anecdotes, riddles, tongue-twisters, rhymes — all representing the play of language;
- selections from newspapers students may not find in their homes, along with articles and reviews from free community newspapers and magazines, online and on the page;
- references such as dictionaries, thesauruses, writing handbooks, books of quotations, online and on the page (I often use references online — quick and filled with information).

Are there differences between "literature" and "literacy"?

I like to think of literature as what we read and literacy as how and why we read. Of course, the texts of our reading lives vary in function and quality, and we can categorize them in so many ways: "classic" texts, popular texts, social media, work-related texts, and so on. But schools generally treat "literature" as texts a library would have included in its collection in the past. The literature canon for youngsters has not altered much over the last forty or fifty years. The same novels are used throughout most school districts in North America, without much awareness of diversity or equity or gender issues, or whether young people are being prepared for a life of literacy. They are often read and analyzed chapter by chapter, with too little attention paid to the impact of this teaching strategy on reader choice and on the future literacy lives of the students. But reluctant readers tell us they want action, raw humour, familiarity, and complex illustrations; in contrast, many teachers prefer elegance of story structure, sophistication of character development, complexity of description, irony, and references to other literature.

What if these readers could find themselves engaged in a powerful book they couldn't put down? What would change in their reading lives? Would they forget their reading difficulties and simply read? Some teachers are able to find the right books for those students who are at a difficult stage in their reading lives. We can try to find resources that connect to their lives: series books like "Junie B. Jones" by Barbara Park (students can read them all and grow in fluency); read-aloud choices like *The Jungle Book* by Rudyard Kipling (classics that we bring to them and are also available in film), and leveled books that still have quality, like Arnold Lobel's "Frog and Toad" series (which works very well with instructional groups).

It may be that some schools will have to bear the burden of literature on their shoulders, that teachers will be the storytellers who reach most children. And yet with the burden come the related strengths that accompany literature in school: curriculum connections; embedded literacy situations; circles of shared experience; modeling of story strength by adults; a sensitivity to authors and illustrators, along with a recognition that the child belongs in this authoring relationship; a wide range of different content, chosen to broaden the child's experiential background, and inclusion of a body of story that carefully and subtly looks at issues of identity, community, sex, race, equity, culture, and so on, that constitutes an exploration of genres and modes that may be unavailable to a child at home; texts by a variety of authors from all over the world, male and female, old and young, books out of print, books hot off the press.

Should I still teach the novel in my classroom?

Absolutely. For many students, novels provide road maps for the difficulties of contemporary life, and they identify with and live through the exploits of the fictitious characters they read about. Often, the teacher can work with novels that the students have read as a class or that a group has read, different novels on a theme, or a novel that has been read aloud to the class over a period of time. Authors seem to understand the needs of students, and there are many fine books from which to choose. Students often enjoy reading several books by a favoured author, or a series of books about a familiar set of characters. Common themes link the most widely read books — humour, school friends, mystery, fantasy — and students should be given as many opportunities as possible for reading independently. Some boys and some girls may prefer different types of books, and yet there are fine novels that, if brought to their attention, will meet their interest needs and present non-sexist portrayals.

Many good novels allow readers to engage in a dialogue with an author on a wide range of topics at a deep emotional level, reflecting their concerns about their place in the adult world, ecology, peace, the future, the past, and any number of other subjects. And a series of books by an author can increase a student's fluency, word recognition, and motivation. Quantity matters in becoming a reader. *Miss Peregrine's Home for Peculiar Children* by Ransom Riggs, *Earth of the Dragons* by Amma Lee, and *The Gods of Asgard* by Rick Riordan, are popular series books, as of course are the Harry Potter novels.

Are graphic texts actual reading texts?

My views on graphic novels were changed when I read *Persepolis*, Marjane Satrapi's memoir of growing up in Iran during the Islamic Revolution and the Iran-Iraq war. I learned so much. Many of today's young readers enjoy reading this type of book, and it shouldn't come as a surprise in a world where visuals from television, videos, games, and computers fill so much of our youngsters' time. In an increasingly image-filled culture, this new literacy medium offers alternatives to traditional texts used in schools, while at the same time promoting literacy development. For many of us, comics are unfortunately tainted as a lesser genre, relegated to childhood's Saturday morning leisure time. But many

Two books that I wrote with Kathy Gould Lundy and Larry Swartz may help teachers wishing to include graphic texts in their literacy programs: *In Graphic Detail: Using Graphic Novels in the Classroom* and *Learning to Read with Graphic Power*.

of today's graphic texts include a complex and art-filled variety of genres, from fiction to biography, social studies, and science, representing social, economic, and political themes and topics that readers might not choose in other types of texts. As well, they present opportunities for incorporating media literacy into the reading program, as students critically examine this word and image medium itself.

Later, I saw the animated film of *Persepolis*, and the two text forms intertwined to give me a lasting emotional response. And I remembered that I had had the largest comic-book collection in my circle in eighth grade.

Examples of graphic books that younger children enjoy include *Lowriders in Space* by Cathy Camper, illustrated by Raúl the Third, *The Arrival* by Shaun Tan, *Big Nate: Welcome to My World* by Lincoln Peirce, and *The Storm in the Barn* by Matt Phelan.

Cameron Smith is a grade-seven student who enjoys drawing and illustrating. Having read the story *Greyling* by Jane Yolen, the print version without pictures, he decided to retell the story in his own words and accompanied by his illustrations to create a graphic book.

Can picture books be used with older students?

Picture books have been my greatest asset in working with students over the years. They are created for the adult to read to the child, and both parties can become involved in the many levels of meaning uncovered by the print and the visual. Read aloud, they pull the class into a community; explored afterwards, they open up opportunities for discussion and deepen understanding. The pictures draw the eye and the text catches the imagination. The words can offer powerful language input for students, new and unusual vocabulary, varied syntactic patterns, strong contextual clues for exploring meaning, characters who struggle with life's problems — sometimes symbolic, sometimes very real. Illustrations in picture books run the gamut of styles and techniques — watercolours, woodcuts, lithography, photography, and collage. They illuminate the text; they extend the words into possibilities of meaning; they shock the reader/listener with new interpretations, lifting the student's own experience into different conceptual realms. The

Steven Layne, in his well-documented and important book *In Defense of Read-Aloud*, offers strong support for continuing to read aloud to our students. Teachers will find techniques for making this time a valuable part of the school program.

old is made new; the new is made relevant. The picture book can be a demanding medium, especially for older readers. Many teachers have shared Shawn Tan's books, such as *The Arrival*, mentioned above, with their older students to great effect, along with *War Game* by Michael Foreman, *Zoo* by Anthony Browne, *FArTHER* by Grahame Baker-Smith, *The Stinky Cheese Man and Other Fairly Stupid Tales* by Jon Scieszka and Lane Smith, *Crow Call* by Lois Lowry, and *Shooting at the Stars: The Christmas Truce of 1914* by John Hendrix. The website Goodreads has lists of great picture books for older students.

Should humour be a part of teaching reading?

As teachers, we don't need to be afraid of texts that make our students laugh. We can help them laugh all the way to the word bank. Many children's and young adult books offer us opportunities for sharing improbable situations and memorable word play experiences with young people. As children laugh at the slapstick and nonsense, the funny and exaggerated characters, or the silly and ridiculous situations, the words and expressions pop up and jiggle the funny bone, and the letters, patterns, and refrains remain in their long-term memories.

Alphabet books, counting books, books of verse, books full of word puzzles, books based on culturally significant sequences such as days of the week or months of the year, books that use recurring patterns from one page to the next: all allow young children to enter the print world with confidence.

Students of all ages love puns and expressions that conjure up amusing images. Riddle and joke books are excellent resources for integrating listening and speaking with reading and writing. Starting the year with such word play, perhaps by pairing children to read a joke book together and then create their own riddle and joke books to share with others, indicates that words and how they go together will be an interesting focus for learning. Encouraging the use of tongue-twisters actively involves students in playing with words and enjoying the sounds of the language. Novels filled with humour will pull many reluctant readers inside, and if there is a series by one author, such as those by Gordon Korman, literacy grows and grows.

How can I make better use of the school library?

Schools with libraries and teacher-librarians are in a unique position to support both teachers and their students. They offer organized resources that can make possible developing curriculum units; they have collections of books and texts (novels, picture books, anthologies, information, poetry, magazines) that can enrich the independent and individualized parts of your programs; they often run the computer labs with instructional software and audio/visual components, such as podcasts and talking books, that you will require for your students; the librarians are aware of what is new both in resources and in professional development, and are assets to team planning. Because they deal with the whole student body, they can assist in cross-grade groupings and present special guests such as children's authors. Today's school libraries are true educational commons, shared spaces for teachers and students to work, learn, and lead within the community.

My grandchildren benefit in their small town from visits by the Bookmobile, a small travelling library that brings new excitement every other week. I remember my classes visiting the public library once a month, and how enriched the students' lives became because the library was within walking distance. If you are relegated to a bookroom without staff, or your own classroom library, begin a volunteer book club (parents would be a great asset) with students, who can help organize and promote the resources available. The Internet has become an invaluable library system for most of us; working with students, we find ways to use this miraculous resource, mindful of the pitfalls and finding ways to incorporate its strengths. I certainly need it.

2

How do I actually teach students to read?

What are the stages of reading development?

The students in our classes reveal a variety of stages of growth as readers and writers. Most children follow what can be considered a continuum of reading acquisition; however, they do not always master skills in order. They may have difficulty with one strategy, yet will have gained another usually demonstrated by a more fluent reader. Of course competencies vary according to the text read and the situation in which the children find themselves. Some classroom books are leveled over approximately three years of literacy growth, but the ages of children able to access a particular book will vary according to experience, background, content of the book, and the students' reading knowledge.

It may be useful to consider how young children move into literacy, and then we can apply that information to older readers, especially those who are struggling with what are labeled as grade-leveled texts.

THE EARLY READER

The early reader begins school with some of the skills and concepts necessary for reading. Many children enjoy experiences with books, having been read to by family members or caregivers. They like to listen to and read with others, and they know that they will be entertained, informed, or amused by books — many children will have favourite stories they like to hear again and again. These readers have a sense of story and enter into it readily.

They will often pick up a book and approximate reading, holding it the right way, stopping the reading while they turn the page, and finishing the story exactly on the last page. Children learn that texts give readers cues to reading, that print on a page matches certain words, that pictures support the story, that books are read from front to back, that text flows from left to right, that reading is an authentic activity. When children "read" books in this way, they are preparing themselves for becoming readers.

THE EMERGENT READER

Emergent readers know that books can provide entertainment and information and they see themselves as capable of reading them. These youngsters have refined their knowledge of how books work, and realize that the purpose of print can be to record or share meaning.

They have a bank of sight words, and are beginning to rely on semantic and syntactic cueing systems to predict words and events, and can retell sequences of events. These children are interested in developing their print abilities. They like to have their stories transcribed, so that they can read them back to the teacher or parent. We need to give them plenty of opportunities to read books successfully, particularly pattern books and books with relevant information.

THE DEVELOPING READER

Children at this stage of reading can read some texts independently and successfully. They often enjoy books by a favourite author, including books in a series, and it is during this period that children come to recognize characteristics of various genres. With this knowledge and their experience in reading, they begin to develop a personal literary taste. Their knowledge of sound-letter correspondence is growing, and they can recognize and write letter groups such as blends and digraphs. Their knowledge of sight words is also growing, and they can read these words in both familiar and unfamiliar contexts. They are able to self-monitor their reading, identifying and correcting miscues, and can substitute words that make sense when they are unsure of a text. At this level, children are reading silently. Some children may still finger point or say the words softly to themselves.

THE FLUENT READER

Fluent readers can read a range of texts for a variety of purposes, read silently, link new information with existing knowledge, and adjust their style of reading to reflect the type of book being read. This is a critical stage in reading. Some children may begin to lose their enthusiasm for reading because books may appear too challenging, or they no longer find themselves as captivated by story. Books need to be motivating and accessible so that children can enjoy them and read them successfully. Fluent readers see reading as an act that entertains them, that brings them satisfaction as well as adding to their knowledge.

THE INDEPENDENT READER

Independent readers read texts independently and silently. The style of reading reflects the material being read, and readers monitor their reading for understanding. These children can read a range of texts that reflect other cultures, other times, and other ways of looking at the world. They are capable of interpreting complex plots and characterization and need to be challenged to move ahead on their own, using both fiction and nonfiction materials and computer texts.

How do I introduce beginning readers to books?

The answers to this question depend upon the students' past experiences, and of course age, home language, and knowledge of how print works. Beginning with one hundred flash cards of function words makes little sense. Rather, I would like us to introduce new books (of high interest) and at a level that the children can explore. We can read the book aloud so that the children are familiar with its style and content and have the opportunity to make personal connections to the text and predictions based on the cover, its title, and illustration. A beginning reader can benefit from sharing a number of predictable, memorable patterned texts, such as *Brown Bear, Brown Bear, What Do You See?* by Bill Martin, Jr. Wordless picture books are an effective literacy tool at all grades. A child can tell the story aloud as he or she turns the pages.

Recently, I brought five-year-old Liam a new picture book, *I Want my Hat Back* by Jon Klassen, when I was invited for dinner. I handed the book to him, and he immediately sat down and began to read it. Ignoring the print code, he began to create dialogue from the picture cues. The surprising revelation was that he was telling the same story, with almost the same dialogue as the words on the pages. Liam knew how books function, how stories work, when characters speak, when actions happen. Later, I read the book to him as he followed along (my favourite method of sharing books with youngsters), bringing the words to life, and chatting about the story.

Children like Liam can soon start reading texts when they feel assured of success and move up gradually. Leveled texts can support a reader's sense of success, as the youngster knows which books can be read without struggling at this stage of literacy development.

Who is involved in "buddy reading"?

An older reader can be a buddy reader to a younger child. The older child finds a book to read during the buddy session and practices it before reading it aloud to the younger child. The opportunity to read to another who will see them as a reader serves as a confidence builder. We are impressed with buddy programs that require the older students to have some training in how to assist their struggling reader, and where they prepare for the session, debrief with the teacher, and even keep a notebook chronicling their progress. Curriculum consultant Amy Robinson writes about her reading mentoring program, which builds on buddy reading:

> The reading mentoring program differs significantly from a traditional reading buddies program. It is more formal, and there is a structure to it. Students in the program are called "mentors" and "partners," which creates a different tone than calling the pairs of students "reading buddies."
>
> In order to remain in touch with the struggling readers and support the mentors, teacher advisers monitor their progress. At each session, we move around the room, listen in to how partners are working together, and often join pairs to model strategies and help mentors to access resources in the manual.
>
> Mentors track what they do. They make a note of what they were working on for that day, the texts that were read, and the strategies they tried. They

You can find a detailed description of the clever plans that Amy Robinson and Lauren Miller have developed for cross-grade tutoring in their article "Reading Rocks: A Reading Mentoring Program," in my book *Caught in the Middle*.

also record ideas for the next session and any questions they have. They hand in this tracking form each week, and teacher advisers provide written descriptive feedback to each of them in order to assist them with their plans for the next session. This aspect of the program lets teacher advisers remain in touch with what each pair is working on.

Are children learning to read and write when they are playing?

One day my granddaughter came home from school and immediately began playing school. With access to markers and paper, she made charts of each of her friends' lunch choices (hot or cold), and sometimes their behaviours (good or not good), attached to each period of the school day. She needed to write, to act literate, freed from judgment.

For me, that is the secret definition of play: we may add structures and specific resources, even timetable events, but the child is agent of his or her own experience. As they engage in playful learning, or learning through play, all kinds of literacy behaviours emerge and become part of their daily lives:

- living alongside books of all kinds and sizes, browsing and noticing how they are used;
- meeting stories told and read aloud, and even better, experiencing the books and the visuals along with the spoken text;
- joining in repetitive phrases and expressions, echoing words, becoming actors in the text;
- representing their new knowledge through role-playing, reinventing and retelling stories, deepening their understanding and their vocabulary;
- sequencing narratives through drama and painting and writing;
- noticing how others react and respond, with similar and different words and actions, interpreting behaviours as readers would;
- making choices, having favourite books, being junior members of the literacy club.

The importance of early childhood literacy experiences is supported in Anne Burke's book *Ready to Learn: Using Play to Build Literacy Skills in Young Learners,* and in Marie Clay's seminal book on Reading Recovery, *An Observation Survey of Early Literacy Achievement.*

What is the most effective kind of phonics instruction?

How can I help students understand how words work?

We want children to enter the world of print with wonder and surprise, reveling in the power and the joy of words. As children use words, play with them, embroider them, taste them on their tongues, and record them on paper, they will become word people who treasure the sounds and visual squiggles that give us language.

Preschool and primary children need to write as often as possible, using their knowledge of how words work to encode their thoughts, using invented spelling at first. They can puzzle over riddle books, laugh at joke books, join in songs and poems, play board games with friends and family. As they grow older, we can examine words used in advertising, slang, jargon, newly coined words, old-fashioned words, expressions from the texts they read, and discover word families and origins. I expand on this in the phonics and spelling sections below.

Is phonemic awareness different from phonics?

Readers and writers require alphabet knowledge, and as children's knowledge of the alphabet builds, so does their awareness of corresponding sounds. Phonemic awareness is the ability to hear, identify, and manipulate individual sounds, called phonemes, in spoken words. Some children find phonemic awareness more difficult than phonics awareness (matching print to sounds). Barring physical challenges that limit auditory discrimination, we can help children to become aware of phonemics through games and patterned books that contain simple structures and vocabulary that support sound-letter awareness. There are dozens of picture books as well as games on line filled with rhymes and rhythms, alphabet fun, puzzles and word play. My favourite phonemic game? "I spy with my little eye, something beginning 'buh,' with the sound of B." And I also keep a collection of alphabet books of every variety.

How should I teach phonics?

Knowing how the print code works is necessary for the reader to make the most meaning possible. Beginning with the alphabet, and using phonemes (units of sound) and morphemes (units of language), we come to learn how words work, how speech is encoded (writing), and how codes are translated as speech (reading aloud). Young skilled code-breakers can often pronounce a word correctly with no understanding of meaning. That is why we try to teach as much as possible about code-breaking with words in context, so the sentence, the punctuation, the storyline, the visuals, help us to add meaning to what we are decoding. If we had to decode all of the words in a passage as we read, we would never finish the reading. Automaticity is required for most words we read in a text.

After the beginning years, children begin to use patterns and analogies that are stored in the brain as their main decoding strategy; words that rhyme, words with similar groups of letters, and morphemes, root words, suffixes, and prefixes. One word you recognize can lead to six or seven others through patterning.

If readers are fairly certain of what a word is, based on information taken from other cues, they can use phonics to analyze the letters and confirm the knowledge. Some children who are having difficulty mastering reading may benefit from focusing on aspects of sound-letter relationships such as consonants, consonant blends and digraphs, and long and short vowel sounds, and then applying this knowledge with actual text. We can support their use of word attack or word-solving skills during guided reading instruction, and during follow-up activities focusing on word knowledge. Sounding out a word can help once in a while during a reading experience, but the larger the segment of groups of letters, the more success with word solving. The reader needs to know the sound of *ph* to decode *phone.* Phonics instruction can help children focus on words while they read, as they unlock letter patterns and sounds to make meaning.

There are excellent programs and books now available for creating phonics activities around games and puzzles, and word knowledge is always useful. For example, as students use invented spelling to write, they are putting their phonic knowledge into action. From these attempts, teachers can readily see their developmental level and where they may benefit from directed teaching. Have no fear of phonics instruction: balance letter-word games and activities with the reading of solid, engaging texts, where young readers can decode unfamiliar words with their knowledge of phonics and context cues, as we adult readers do.

I still return to Patricia Cunningham's writings for help with the complex issues of the best ways to handle phonics: *Phonics They Use: Words for Reading and Writing* (6th Edition).

Some of the ways in which students can explore how words work are games of Concentration (matching pairs of words with common features) and grouping words that share a pattern (e.g., onsets and rhymes, blends, digraphs, or silent letters).

- Students can find a word that sounds like — — — ; find a word that follows alphabetically; find an opposite or similar word, and so on.
- Students can use word sorts to categorize words:
    words with recurring patterns (double letters);
    words that rhyme;
    words with the same number of syllables;
    words with silent letters.

What are sight words, word walls, and word banks?

How should children learn sight words?

When I arrived to pick up my son at the sitter's home one evening, he was sitting on the couch with the sitter's younger daughter, both of them staring into space. I subsequently learned that Laura and her mom and dad had been attempting to get her to complete her homework in first grade — sight recognition of ten words that she just couldn't seem to remember. After a futile hour and a half, Mom was upstairs crying, Dad had retreated to the basement, and the children were staring straight ahead. I took down the ten words that had been taped to the living-room wall, found some blank file cards, and asked Laura to tell me ten words that she could read, and I wrote them on the cards. *Fluffy — the cat*; *Jay — friend*; and so on. I taped the cards to the wall, and I said she had finished her homework. Learning to read must not be painful, for the child, the instructor, or the parents.

Most children recognize their name as their first sight word. To me, it makes more sense to focus on names and labels in building a recognizable sight-word list, rather than function words that can't be seen in the mind's eye. By the time most children arrive in school they will have some sight-word knowledge, including environmental print (e.g., fast-food signs) and some words in stories that have been read aloud to them.

To read print effectively, a reader has to recognize words quickly, accurately, and easily, with as little effort as possible while reading. Not surprisingly, as children engage in activities that promote fluency (e.g., rereading, partner reading, choral reading) they begin to recognize words quickly and accurately. As they are exposed to words and word chunks that appear often in text, they begin to respond automatically, which helps them to focus on concepts and ideas, and decode the occasional new unfamiliar word as they read. The larger the sight-word vocabulary, the easier the reading experience. Encountering a number of difficult words is frustrating for a developing reader, and extra preparation may be required when materials have specialized or uncommon vocabulary. Recognizing frequently used words should ultimately be automatic, not requiring phonetic sounding out, so that children can spend their time and energy decoding and understanding less frequently used words.

The title of their book *Word Nerds: Teaching All Students to Love Vocabulary* underscores the valuable information presented by Brenda Overturf, Leslie Montgomery, and Margot Holmes-Smith, and encourages us to find effective ways of promoting vocabulary growth in our students.

What do word walls offer students?

A word wall — a large visual display of words — acts as an immediate, accessible class reference and supports student' reading and writing. Word walls should always be associated with significant activities where the words that students need are accessible. Words can be changed when necessary, and act as a reference for students' writing, and for curriculum topics. if the class is studying plants in spring, and writing observations and descriptions and creating diagrams of the seeds sprouting, they can use displayed words such as *habitat, life cycle, leaves, stem, stalk, roots, blossoms, chlorophyll.*

You can select words from a book they are reading, from functional words they may need, from big ideas, or from inquiries and themes they are exploring. These can be referred to when students are reading or writing. Students can group the words into useful categories, highlight them with boxes or colours, and add and delete them as necessary.

Should each student have a personal word bank?

Word banks give children ownership and investment in the words they learn, increasing their interest and enthusiasm for learning in general. Students choose key words from their reading, record the words on index cards, and file them in a personal word bank. Because the students own their banks, they recognize their words more easily. The teacher may add complementary words to the bank to emphasize concepts (e.g., sound-letter relationships), but it is the students who ultimately control their banks and the words in them. I like children to write each word they know in a "life words" book, the words that will support their literacy lives — family names, food they like, sports heroes, favourite toys and television shows. Soon they will have one hundred words they can recognize in print.

How do I build a wide vocabulary with my students?

I am always surprised by the words that young students have absorbed from media and from listening to adults talking. We want to promote this active engagement with the new words students are experiencing in their homes and communities, and to bring them new and unusual words as we read and talk together, as they question, explore, and interact with the texts they are reading, as we read aloud to them, as we discover new terms in our research and study. The more children read on their own, the more meanings they gain and remember. The more extensive a reader's vocabulary, the easier it is for the reader to understand unfamiliar texts. The more varied the language experiences children have, the more words and expressions they will master. Words must matter in order to remain in our long-term memories. We remember words that we need and want to use.

Mara, age seven, is reading the Harry Potter books, with all the British expressions in them. She first heard the books read by her mother, and then after finishing each one in the series, they watched the film version together. Now those words are firmly ensconced in her reading repertoire. By seeing difficult or unfamiliar words in a variety of texts, students can apply their knowledge of word decoding to make meaning from unknown words. The more children read, the more familiar the words become, and the more efficient is their subsequent recognition of those words. They begin to see themselves as effective readers.

When my nephew Frankie was five, he was rapidly becoming technology-wise, with access to the family computer, his own website, and excitement about his Internet searches. After returning home from a shopping trip to the mall with his mother, he said, "I need to go upstairs and put a new word in my word bank on my computer." The word was "infestation." When he had noticed a display of decorative butterflies hanging from the ceiling of a department store, his mother had mentioned that there was an "infestation of butterflies." This fascinating word was remembered all the way home and added to his word bank as a permanent piece of vocabulary.

Students gain new sight words through extensive reading and follow-up discussion to ensure that the words become integrated into their personal discourse. Teaching lists of new words out of context has little or no potential for increasing vocabulary for most students. They can use texts that are memorable (such as rhymes and rhythms), those that follow predictable patterns, and series like Arnold Lobel's "Frog and Toad" in which the same words are repeated. They can, as well, read their own compositions and teacher-generated texts that highlight or repeat core words. As well, students can have fun with words — newly coined words, archaic words, palindromes, collective nouns, and so on. For example, they could match an animal to an appropriate collective name (there are dozens of sites online with sample lists):

herd	*beavers*
army	*bees*
culture	*ants*
colony	*bacteria*
lodge	*antelope*

How do I increase reading fluency, both silent and oral?

Connected join-in, participatory, out-loud sessions with texts involve readers in the sounds of language, and poems, songs, scripts, and chants cause them to read the words aloud, building fluency and word power. These selections can support and increase fluency with repetition and rhyme, careful chunking of words and phrases, and suggestions for joining in and rereading.

Fluency depends on a variety of factors: familiarity with the text, the context for the reading, the mastery of the vocabulary, and the self-worth the student demonstrates as a reader. Singing a song with the lyrics provided with copies or on the board or a screen is my favourite way to open discussions of fluency; we all need to keep pace together, and the tune provides the means for fluent reading.

When good readers read aloud fluently, they use phrasing to communicate their meaning. When they read silently, they interpret the text and add it to their knowledge base. Less fluent readers, on the other hand, tend to read at the same speed, no matter what the text, both silently and orally, and use the same phrasing, even calling out each word. They may not use all of the syntactic cues a text provides or the many factors that contribute to comprehension (e.g., punctuation, syntactic structures).

In repeated readings, a child can practice reading one passage several times until she or he can read it fluently. The benefits of repeated readings are numerous, particularly for at-risk readers, and carry over to other texts that they have not practiced, helping to increase fluency, word recognition, and comprehension.

The well-known educator Regie Routman tells of a student who said that her first reading of a book was like a rough draft of her writing.

For some students, hearing an oral version of the text gives them the confidence to read it. Using a number of commercial programs that present the text orally alongside the printed text can benefit readers who do not yet recognize the flow of visual language.

How do reading strategies help students comprehend texts?

As readers, we often consciously or unconsciously employ a variety of strategies as we attempt to read a complicated text: we might read some background information beforehand; we might read between the lines to deepen our understanding; we might make connections as we read to other texts like this one, or reread a passage to make sense of some new information. With our students, we can take the time to draw attention to a particular strategy by focusing on how readers make use of it, and present activities that demonstrate its use to us as readers. When I was introducing my book *The Dust Bowl* to junior students in a school library, I had prepared PowerPoint slides of images from the Internet of the 1930s in the Midwest, and I chatted with the students about some of the statistics and conditions. As I read my book to them, they had images of the people and places so sorely affected by weather and trouble, and their belief in my characters was deepened.

How can students enrich comprehension before reading?

Many things affect how a reader makes sense of a particular text: knowledge of the content of the selection from background experience; familiarity with the author's writing style or other similar books; an understanding of the issues or the context of the selection, and the reason for reading it. When we spend time with students before their reading, especially with material that is unfamiliar, we will help ensure that the reading becomes a more meaningful and satisfactory experience. We can help students build and activate their background knowledge so that they can integrate the new print text with what they already know. Pre-reading activities can arouse students' curiosity and give them a purpose for reading. We may teach some vocabulary, which we call focus words, but only a few words necessary for understanding the content and context of the story, since students need to learn to identify and solve words from context. The more we know about a topic, the greater our background experience, and the easier it is for us to connect to a topic. For homework, Laura was reading *To Kill a Mockingbird*, with dozens of "comprehension" questions to be answered. In chatting with her, I found she had little knowledge of the history of racism and civil unrest in the US, She was missing the core of the conflict in the book. I found two copies of Rosa Parks's story: first I read the picture book *Rosa* by Nikki Giovanni to her, and she then read *Rosa Parks: My Story*, by Rosa Parks and Jim Haskins. Book sets are often the best way to enlarge backgrounds and to then deepen comprehension of an unfamiliar text.

How can students monitor and maintain comprehension while reading?

We now recognize that many students need support while they are reading, not just after they have completed a passage. Many factors affect the understanding of a text or the ability to continue reading it: the context in which the students are reading (peer group pressure, the physical setting), the purpose of the reading (scientific information, fiction), and supportive assistance (discussing a complex format, clarifying an unfamiliar phrase). We can encourage comprehension during the reading through directed, guided reading sessions with a small group, or working with an individual student. We want to help readers use their reading strategies, build meaning and comprehension, and practice word-solving skills as they read, and we can focus on one strategy at a time, even though they will all work together in a text.

1. Making connections to reading: life connections, text connections, world connections

Our main goal as literacy teachers must be to help students build bridges between the ideas in a text and their own lives, helping them to access the prior knowledge relevant to making meaning with the text, the information that the brain has retained and remembered, sometimes accompanied by emotional responses or visual images. When we help students enhance their reading by activating their own connections, we offer them a reading strategy for life.

We can help students to begin to recognize text-to-text connections by selecting particular text sets to be used during independent reading or literature circles: books selected by common themes or writing styles; books about the same characters or events; several books by the same author; or different versions of the same story. Comparisons and contrasts offer us a simple means of noting text-to-text connections. As students see other relationships among texts, we can record these on a chart, even formally rewriting them as a reminder to be aware of making connections as we read. The class can connect texts by issues, themes, setting, characters, time period, story lines, mood, style, or genre.

During a reading time with three hundred students organized for an author celebration in a school library, I had chosen to read aloud *Greyling* by Jane Yolen, and during the response time after the story, I casually asked if anyone knew other stories about foundlings or changelings, and one by one they offered tales they had met in their young experiences, of babies found in tree stumps, in bushes, in shells, in leaves, filling the room with story memories, and increasing their knowledge of how folklore has worked for hundreds of years.

I am grateful to educator Paulo Freire for giving us the expression "reading the word, reading the world." Somehow, when we read powerful, significant texts, we travel outside ourselves, exploring what lies beyond our immediate neighbourhood, extending our vision, and encouraging our personal meaning-making.

Kelly Gallagher's book *In the Best Interest of Students: Staying True to What Works in the ELA Classroom* presents excellent teaching/learning experiences for engaging older students in authentic literacy and literature events.

I want my students to work through "What does the text say?" and "What does the text mean?" as soon as possible so they can spend as much time as possible applying their newfound thinking toward answering, "How does this book make me smarter about today's world?" I want them to deeply consider what the books *mean in our world and for their future.*

Kelly Gallagher, *In the Best Interest of Students*

The picture book *Encounter* by Jane Yolen is a powerful way to introduce the complicated stories of European explorers arriving in North America. Columbus's story is told from the viewpoint of a young Taino boy on the island of San Salvador seeing the explorers arrive. Students' perceptions are altered, and the "other" is now present in the story. The tale of Columbus is altered forever.

2. Making inferences and predictions while reading

We spend our lives making inferences, noting all the signs that help us to make sense of any experience — the face of the salesclerk displaying a product, weekend weather reports, the body language of the students we are teaching. As readers or viewers, we make inferences when we go beyond the literal meaning of the text, whether it is a film, a speech, or a book, and begin to examine the implied meanings, reading between the lines. When we read, our connections drive us to infer; we struggle to make sense of the text, looking into our minds to explain what isn't on the page, building theories that are more than just the words. We conjecture while we are reading, the information accrues, our ideas are modified, changed, or expanded as this new text is added to our store of knowledge and experience. Designing an activity that encourages inferring, and then helping students to notice the process in action, may demonstrate how we can use this strategy in our reading. You can choose a picture book to share with the class, and as you read it aloud, pause as students reveal the inferences they are making. You can offer prompts, such as:

- Why are the characters behaving in this way?
- What did the character really mean by what she said?
- What do you think might happen next?
- What is the author really saying here?
- What does this story remind you of?
- What are the big ideas or themes in this text?

3. Visualizing what is happening in the text

This is about imagining what we are reading. Words are only symbols, a code for capturing ideas and feelings. When I was growing up, I listened to radio dramas and comedies, where the airwaves delivered the images to my mind, aided by sound effects, the narrator, and the actors. When we read, a similar process occurs, and we create pictures of what the print suggests, making movies in our heads. Each of us builds a visual world unlike any other. Our imaginations are at work. We can demonstrate this strategy for youngsters and help make them aware of its strength in supporting our meaning-making with print texts. We might read a folktale to students and then have them share the mental images they created throughout the listening experience. They could draw images suggested by the text. Reflecting upon the meanings suggested by an artist's illustration can be an effective means of demonstrating visualization and the need to reconsider our thoughts as we learn more. This is why graphic novels can be a stimulus for young readers to begin seeing in their minds what the print conjures for them.

Reading the Visual: An Introduction to Teaching Multimodal Literacy by Frank Serafini strengthens our awareness of including visual texts in our literacy programs.

The images that form in your mind as you read — we call them "brain movies" — can be more exciting and memorable than a Hollywood film. More to the point for teachers, guiding your students to visualize as they read is an engaging and enjoyable way to boost comprehension and retention.

Donna Wilson and Marcus Conyers, www.brainsmart.org

4. Synthesizing and summarizing information and ideas while reading

Stephanie Harvey and Anne Goudvis, in their helpful book *Strategies That Work*, write that "synthesizing involves putting together assorted parts to make a new whole." We synthesize the issues and ideas generated by our reading of a text in light of our own lives. When we synthesize, we change what we thought we knew — we expand our personal understanding. We move from recounting the new information into rethinking our own constructs of the world. We synthesize our new learning in order to consider the big ideas that affect our lives.

The more we connect the bits and pieces of print information with our previous experiences, the greater the chance of finding new patterns and of developing deeper insights.

Retelling a story can assist in helping children to use this strategy of synthesizing to get to the significant issues. As they compare retellings, they can begin to notice the weight each teller places on the different aspects of the story as they personalize their versions. We can list common themes found in the retellings on a chart, showing how we all struggle to move to the universal truths as we share narratives. It may help to have the children write a synthesis of the story they can then read aloud, and to have them find supportive information for their choices.

5. Determining and prioritizing ideas

My own books are full of different-coloured self-adhering stick-it notes; they hang out from the tops, bottoms, and sides of almost every book on my shelves. Why haven't I made the teaching/learning connection and begun using these markers with students of all ages? As readers, we have to read a text, think about it, and make conscious decisions about what we need to remember and learn. Sorting significant information from less important information means picking out the main ideas and noticing supporting details.

Traditionally, we have taught students that finding the main idea was the first step in understanding a text. Sometimes we meant a plot summary; other times we wanted to find a theme. Now we know that this is not a simple process, that there may be many ideas in a reading selection. What we need to do is assist young readers in learning how to determine what is important (especially in nonfiction material), what is necessary and relevant to the issues being discussed and what can be set aside.

For example, there is seldom any useful reason for finding the answers to a series of questions that ask students to locate or, even worse, to remember insignificant details from a novel. What we use in constructing meaning are the pieces of information that add to our growing understanding of what we want to find out or are ready to experience; these are details we can't do without, pieces of the puzzle necessary for creating the complete picture. The question has to be this: Which details matter? In my own teaching, I try not to ask a student to locate a detail unless that piece of information is necessary for a deeper understanding of what is being explored. I want the student to search out the facts necessary for understanding, for supporting an idea or clarifying a point, not to rely on a treasure hunt for details that I determine to be important.

3

Should students always respond to a text?

How do I know if a response activity is a meaningful one?

What's wrong with designing a new book cover? What's wrong with book reports? When is it okay to do nothing with a book that the students have read? These questions are all about responding to what has been read, but unless the activity is part of a test, we can help students explore their personal responses after reading inside, outside, and all around the text.

Rather than answering a dozen questions on character details, or recounting the plot, students can come to see how their responses are opening up the questions and concerns they themselves discovered through their reading of the text. If students write reports as an outgrowth of the reading and the subsequent reflection that grew from conversations with fellow readers about the text, or from thoughtful reflections drawn from their reading journals, then these can help students consider the text in light of the experiences surrounding it — a far cry from simplistic statements such as "I liked it" or "I didn't like it."

By incorporating a variety of response activities, we can move students into different, divergent, critical, and deeper levels of thinking, feeling, and learning. We can discover with our students what they think they read and saw and heard and felt in their experience with the text, helping them come to grips with their own and others' perceptions; they have a chance to rethink and rework their initial reactions. Their printed or visual responses as they write and create through visual art, the conversations that grow from their book clubs, or the students' research online about the time or place of the story, make them active and involved agents in making sense of what they have experienced and reveal how they are affected by their reading. Through authentic responses, they can question the text, uncover biases, and connect issues to their own lives, cultures, and communities. When we allow and encourage student responses, the voice of every reader or viewer can be represented on issues of social justice, gender, faith, and culture. This valuing of personal response, expanded and rethought by insightful activities, can open the reading process for young minds who may not be voluntarily engaged by the literacy period. If they can connect personally to the texts they encounter, drawing on their backgrounds and their experiences, they can become agents of their own learning.

What is meant by "close reading" of a text?

With a grade-six class in Manhattan, I read aloud from the overhead screen Jane Yolen's very short story "The Promise."

> Deep in the forest she waited.
> Not even a stray wind broke the silence.
> When she heard footsteps, she looked up,
> sighing deeply,
> not caring the hunters heard,
> her long wait over.
> When the blanched, weary girl sat,
> the unicorn gratefully moved
> forward, putting her head into the promised lap.

Because its brevity surprised them, I read the text aloud again. (It seems that many students wait to tune in until they think it is necessary; by then, this story is over.) We discussed the text in small groups and then shared our findings. The problem lay in connecting what they knew about unicorns with this truncated tale filled with incongruities. The students struggled to make sense of the ideas, examining every word and detail to try and build a larger picture that held together. They visualized, questioned, analyzed details, all in their attempts to find out what the story could mean to us who were reading it in that classroom. They used bits of information from films, cartoons, books, illustrations, and history.

One student reexamined the title, wondering who had made the promise and to whom, when suddenly a boy blurted out, "What if the girl had promised the searchers? What if she was a decoy sent to trap the unicorn?" This caused much discussion and eventually most of the class accepted this point of view, supporting it with details from the story. But three holdouts felt no girl would betray a mythical beast, and felt certain the unicorn had promised to remain with the girl.

Fifty minutes of thoughtful discussion were drawn from a fifty-word story. Most of the students were using their connections from life, from stories, and from the text itself to synthesize information about unicorns, hunters, and girls, and to construct for themselves a shocking new image of medieval archetypes, altering their unicorn worlds forever. And even the three holdouts were comparing their versions of what might be with their classmates, and nervously and stubbornly hanging on.

Close reading can be a demonstration of the complex negotiation of meaning among the reader, the text, and the context of the experience. It is but one tool in our teaching kit.

Which questions are more important —
the students' or the teacher's?

Do I need to ask questions when students have finished reading a text?

Often our most limited readers ask themselves the fewest questions as they read, waiting for us to interrogate them when they have finished the disenfranchising ritual of the prescribed print offering. They have not learned that confusion is allowed as we read, that in fact authors count on it in order to build the dynamic that compels us to continue reading.

We read because we are curious about what we will find; we keep reading because of the questions that fill our reading minds. Of course, good readers ask questions before they read, as they read, and when they are finished. As we become engaged with a text, questions keep popping up, questions that propel us to predict what will happen next, to challenge the author, to wonder about context for what is happening, to fit the new information into our world picture. We try to rectify our confusion, filling in missing details, attempting to fit into a pattern all the bits and pieces that float around our meaning-making, even reflecting back on our own experiences. We continue to read because the author has made us curious, and this constant self-questioning causes us to interact with the text, consciously and subconsciously. As we read on, our questions may change, and the answers we seek may lie outside the print. Not all of our questions will be answered during the reading of a text. And as we continue to read or reread, we can sometimes clarify the confusion or resolve the difficulty as we gain more insight into the text, making inferences as we try to make sense.

Of course I have questions to ask, but they will grow from our conversations about the text, from the honest revelations of the students' own concerns, as I try to guide them into deeper interpretations. But now I attempt to ask questions that are driven by their inquiring dialogue, as I would in a conversation with peers during a book club session, based on my listening to their interactions rather than to my own scripted agenda. I like the description Gay Su Pinnell and Irene Fountas give in their book *Guiding Readers and Writers* for using this strategy: "The teacher's questions are a light scaffold that helps students examine text in new ways."

We can reveal how we teachers ask ourselves questions throughout the reading experience by demonstrating the process, writing down the questions that come up in a shared piece of print. This public monitoring of our own reading can often teach and free student readers to recognize how interacting with text works, and it may even free some of them from their own restrictive patterns of regarding the text as a frozen maze that remains insoluble.

I now tend to use prompts rather than recall questions in my interactions with students during group sessions and individual conferences, and in responses to their reading and writing notebooks. These prompts may expand or deepen the offerings of the students, helping them clarify or expand their thoughts, and nudging them into expressing their own questions, sharing opinions and ideas. We have questions to ask and we need to ask them, but we want to teach our students to ask their own, to behave as proficient readers do, framing personal and public questions to promote deeper understanding of the ideas stimulated by the text.

How important are student-generated questions?

As teachers, we will need to ask questions at times, during instructional periods, with mini-lessons, or while conducting a science experiment. However, as we have seen, during inquiry planning or group discussions about novels, students need opportunities to bring their own questions to the table. We have a much greater chance of having our students invest themselves in the reading experience if we help them to take ownership of their own puzzlements. They may begin to participate in text-inspired meaning-making if they believe that their questions really matter, and that others are interested in grappling with them. When we as teachers are solely responsible for asking all the questions, there is little chance that many students will be engaged in a rigorous negotiation of the text and their inquiries. Chris Tovani in her book *I Read It, But I Don't Get It* says, "Forging paths of new thinking is discouraged when students aren't allowed to cultivate uncertainties." Struggling readers can begin to take control over their own reading as they raise questions that matter to them and search for answers themselves.

All of Cris Tovani's books are helpful in seeing how we can help older students learn to comprehend different texts in different subjects. I still return to *I Read It But I Don't Get It*; the title says it all.

After I'd read the story "The Seal Mother" to sixty junior students, their hands went up immediately with all kinds of questions. But their main concern was the unfair treatment of the seal mother, half-human, half-seal, who could only see her children once a year:

> **Student 1**: She can never come back to the land again.
> **Student 2:** That's not fair. She will have to see her children on the rocks by the sea once a year.
> **Student 3:** The children will feel abandoned by their mother. They will only have a single parent.
> **Student 1:** To see their mother on a rock in the sea is sick!
> **Student 4:** A mother should have the right to see her children anywhere she wants.
> **Students:** Yeah!

As we can see in the transcript above, student emotions ran high as they voiced their responses to the story. The students struggled to make sense of complex issues drawn from folklore, and felt compelled to add their own resolutions, which they did, inventing a vaccine that would prevent any sea disease from being spread to the other villagers. This wasn't where I'd expected the class to go, but it was every bit as rich as my ideas for response.

How can I use a reading journal in my program?

I so enjoy reading the journals and responses of students at every stage of their growth, from first grade to graduate school. The personal voice seems to add a stronger dimension to their comments, insights, and questions. In reading journals the students can communicate their thoughts and feelings about the texts they are reading. They begin with their "in the head" responses as they read, their affective reactions to the impact of the selection. Then the students can become more reflective about the text, returning to it and rereading their initial responses. They may at the end keep a list of the books they have read, and they may include sketches or charts that support their responses.

Nancie Atwell's classic book *In the Middle* outlines a rich program using literature to support literacy development.

What types of comments should I make in my students' reading journals?

Educator Nancie Atwell taught us to read and respond to five journals each day, covering the class in a week. Reading the journals allows you to interact with each student in a conversation as an interested person, and then as a teacher. You can offer genuine comments and opinions so that your message connects with the student's in some way:

- You can pose questions that involve rethinking or rereading on the part of the reader.
- You can share your own experiences as a reader and writer, the authors and books you enjoy. You can question things that you don't understand or that the student has not clarified.
- You can ask for more information for a particular interpretation.
- You can recommend other authors or titles or genres, or books with similar themes or events.
- You can try to have an authentic conversation even if you haven't read the student's book by valuing the student's responses and acknowledging their thoughts and feelings.
- You can ask questions that draw your students out in more personal ways and learn more about them as readers and writers and as people.

Here is a part of teacher Nancy Steele's response to a student's entry on Phillip Pullman's *The Amber Spyglass*, annotations added:

> Have you ever thought of the ethical component of these teen sci-fi/fantasy books? [*raising issues connected with the text*] You mention that the "dust" seems to have some relationship to good and evil but it is ambiguous. [*drawing attention to the unusual symbolism of a word in the text*] Do you think that Pullman is dealing with the theme of good and evil? So many sci-fi fantasy writers are. Madeleine L'Engle, whom I know you have read, has a very strong Judeo-Christian element in most of her books and most often the conflict involves destroying the agents of evil. [*directing the student into other texts with similar themes*] Thanks.

Does storytelling belong in a literacy program?

One of the most valuable prompts that we can use when a student has finished reading a story is, "Tell me about your story." As the student becomes a story-teller, we tune in to their personal hoard of words, ideas, stories, songs, and concepts, as they deepen their understanding and appreciation of text. As well, we can engage students in telling and retelling narratives in dozens of ways, from games involving taking turns as storytellers to more formal occasions where a student has prepared a story to share with a class or with a younger group.

In her book *And None of It Was Nonsense*, Betty Rosen told of her work with ESL secondary students in England. She had them tell stories from their own cultural backgrounds, honing them, retelling them, reworking them into polished pieces, artifacts of their own lives. They shared their stories as a classroom community, representing different cultures and countries, and their fluency in English grew alongside their presentational skills. They became storytellers of their own lives.

My friend and colleague Bob Barton is a professional storyteller who can weave a tale that catches two hundred students at a time in its web. These are a few of his suggestions for beginning the storytelling process:

- As the storyteller spins the tale, the teacher may signal for someone to continue the story, or another student may choose to continue on his or her own at a dramatic pause in the story. A "talking stick" is held by each student when it is his or her turn to speak, and is passed on to the next student when the speaker stops (sometimes in mid-phrase).
- In a larger group, the teacher tells an improvised story, pauses every so often, and points to someone in the group to add an appropriate word. "Once upon a time there was a young..." "He walked until suddenly..." "He said ... "
- Begin a round-robin storytelling activity by dividing the class into small groups and asking each person in a group to read the same story silently. When students have finished, number them off. On a prearranged signal, student 1 from each group begins to retell until the signal sounds. Student 2 takes over, then student 3, and so on (in this way the story is retold with no one person being entirely responsible).
- Students can tell stories in a circle, with a partner, through mime and tableau, chorally, or as narration for mime. They can improvise from the story, change the story, or find new stories within the story.
- Using picture books without text, students can describe in their own words what they see happening, sometimes supplying the characters with what they feel is appropriate dialogue.

Storytelling from a point of view

I enjoy having students retell a shared story by selecting a character from or around the story, and retelling the story from the point of view of that character. So many interesting points arise as the student assumes a stance as the in-role teller. You as teacher can follow the same process, adopt a role, and tell part or all of the narrative. Students can work in pairs or groups as well:

- Reporter: Here is what I have chosen to tell about.
- Witness: I was there and I saw it all.
- Friend: I need to tell you what happened to my friend.
- Gossip: You won't believe what I just heard.
- Leader: Listen, my people! You must understand what I will tell you.
- Therapist: Your problems will be revealed in this story I will tell you.
- Police officer: Here is what happened, Your Honour.
- Government bureaucrat: This story is the official word of the government.
- Conscience: What fills my mind as I tell the story?
- Alien: How amusing! This story would not happen in my world.
- Patient: After I tell this story, you will know what happened to me.
- Family member: This story has been passed down in our family.
- Seer: I will tell you a story and it will come true.
- Spirit: I want to tell you the story. Can you see or hear me?
  Robot: I have recorded what has happened and I will play it back.

Absolutely, in every grade. We read aloud what we've written, excerpts from other stories that we loved or wondered about, words that touch us or puzzle us, tales from before, stories about today and tomorrow, episodes from peoples' lives, poems that cry out for sounds in the air, letters from friends, stories about places where we have never wandered, stories about dogs and horses and mothers and granddads and eccentrics and students and school and city and countryside, stories of hope and death and wonder and fantasy. We read aloud short stories and long stories and chapters that build up the tension for days. We read aloud stories from album covers and music sheets, blurbs about writers from the backs of book jackets, titles, reviews, and recommendations. We fill the classroom with the voices of our ancestors, our friends, our novelists, our poets, our records, our documents, our indigenous people, our researchers, our journalists, our ad writers.

Think-alouds

Throughout the year, we can use our time for reading aloud or viewing films as an opportunity for think-aloud sessions as a community. We can share our own reading strategies as we read aloud and think aloud in classroom demonstrations with a common text. Students can see how we construct meaning in a variety of ways with different types of texts, how we continue to grow as readers. We want our students to notice us as readers, how we function within the culture of literacy, and we want to be aware of our own thinking and strategies with print, how we handle confusion and breakdowns when reading.

When we demonstrate our own thinking out loud, we make our thinking visible to our students, so that they can see how we handle a piece of text, before we read, while we are reading, and after we read. When students have opportunities to see our processes in action, they may be able use these strategies in their own work.

It is helpful to choose a text that is easily accessed, so that students can focus on the reading strategies. Select a short text that will enable you to say aloud what you are thinking as you read it through. You might begin with a passage that you have thought through first or use a sight piece that will give the students an authentic picture of how readers read. You can share the text on a chart or SMART Board. Choose a selection that will focus on a particular strategy that you feel the students need.

How many read-aloud experiences can you create for students?

- rereading a story the whole class loves;
- playing recordings and films of authors and artists reading stories;
- having retired volunteers share books with young audiences;
- having older students read to younger buddies;
- having groups of students prepare a story for an audience of their peers;
- reading a story as a monologue where you take on the persona of a character;
- finding a new version of a well-known story;
- sharing a brand-new book by an admired author or illustrator;
- reading a story that requires the help of the participating audience to come alive;
- reading under a tree in the playground on a hot June afternoon.

What and when should students read orally?

Oral reading by students is often a problem for me, unless it is one-on-one assessment with the teacher. An observation assessment can be very useful, using a running record as in Reading Recovery, or a miscue analysis record. However, I find it difficult to watch a struggling reader staggering through a book for the teacher (or parent), every word a puzzle piece that doesn't fit his picture, frustration mounting, and the adult jumping on his every attempt at pronouncing a word. But the smiles that cross the face of a child reading a text he owns, secure in his knowledge of the words and the story, predicting alongside the predictable text, following the clever patterns set out by the author, laughing at the juxtaposition of the funny visuals and the lines; these experiences are so worthwhile, and of course they build literacy success. Too often, students are saying the words, but missing the sense.

Oral reading practice in a group can result in little or no comprehension for limited or struggling readers, as they wait their turn and focus only on pronunciation. These students need to employ word-solving strategies as they read silently and then interpret the words aloud. Do we help with the difficult words? Yes, if they need us to, even when they're accomplished readers. My granddaughter Mara, age seven, was reading aloud to me Roald Dahl's *Charlie and the Chocolate Factory*, a book she had enjoyed before. Whenever she came to an unfamiliar British term, she would use her formidable word-solving skills and pronounce it almost correctly. When I would quietly suggest the standard pronunciation, she would say, "Wow! Was I ever close!" or something along that line. On she would read, finding new discoveries in her rereading, one of the main reasons for sharing texts with others.

Without opportunity to interrogate the text, to rub up against it, to notice how others are feeling and wondering, to question private belief, to expand information, and to hear the voices of print struggling for freedom, the student will be sharing print aloud for no real reason. A few students can decode phonetically and comprehend almost nothing. These kids especially need occasion for coming to grips with the meat of the story before attempting to share their knowledge. The teller and the told are each precious in this process of reading aloud. Sometimes, it is the reader who is also listening, learning through the ear and the eye at the same time.

Discovering oral reading events that move students forward with satisfaction is a hobby of mine:

- They can be part of the choral speaking of poems and rhythmic stories, safely hidden from the critical ears of those who might hinder the process.
- They can read their own writings aloud in small groups, poems that touch them, excerpts that make connections, quotations from novels that represent universal truths, personal writings from journals or writing folders.
- They can work with a buddy from an older class, someone who will offer an experienced shoulder to lean on as they read to each other.
- They can read aloud sentences, phrases, and words that are useful in proving a point during story discussion, to support their own ideas and viewpoints.
- They can read aloud in an assessment situation, one on one with the teacher or diagnostician, without rehearsal and without the embarrassment of peers listening in.

- Perhaps different groups have explored various aspects of a theme or topic, and want to hear from each other to expand their knowledge.
- They can read aloud inside the drama frame, through role play: excerpts, statements, findings, letters, documents, tales, and scripts.
- Readers theatre is a technique that allows students to dramatize narration — selections from novels, short stories, picture books, poems — instead of reading aloud scripted material.

Is choral reading the same as singing songs together?

In some ways, they are similar. Both groups read aloud a shared text having explored the nature of the selection — the themes, the language, the choices the group makes about how to interpret the words, how the words will be spoken or sung. Choral reading, however, belongs to the world of theatre, where the spoken word creates a sense of drama. For example, a few years ago, I was invited to take part in an annual conference in Detroit. Rather than addressing the delegates, though, I was to work with local students. The organizing committee felt that a conference devoted to reading should begin with an event dedicated to the students who might benefit from it. It was decided that there should be a participatory reading experience followed by a circus performance: I was to conduct the former, and Ringling Bros. and Barnum & Bailey Circus would provide the latter.

I hesitated to accept the offer. The sheer number of students — more than three thousand — was daunting. The challenge proved too intriguing, though, and I found myself in an open-air arena on the banks of the Detroit River with thousands of students in front of me and a microphone in my hand. I had decided to tell an African story that involved four different chants, and had distributed copies of the chants beforehand, each on a different-coloured sheet of paper. At the appropriate time, I would call out, "Pink Papers" or "Green Papers," and those students with the right papers would provide the required response. I had not counted on the volume of the chanting, and the response was overwhelming. With thousands of students chanting and clapping on cue, the story took on the attributes of a ritual.

As I was nearing the end, I looked up, and around the amphitheatre stood the circus people and animals — clowns, acrobats, elephants — all drawn by the chorus, watching the performance of the students, a setting by Fellini. For me, it was a powerful event, where reading aloud was completely embedded in story, and where story was alive and well, being lived at the moment by three thousand students.

I am so pleased when I see teachers discovering the power of shared reading. The strategies required for interpreting text orally and together will support the students in their own reading forever. As a young teacher, I attended the monthly in-service sessions run by language arts supervisor Bill Moore. He would present us with several poems for shared choral reading that we could take back to our classrooms. As he took us through them, modeling the reading with his deep and mellifluous British accent, the hairs on the back of my neck stood up with the excitement this foreshadowed with my own grade seven and eight students. The class and I did every one: the funny ones, the moody ones, the ones with long words that fooled our tongues, the Scottish ballads, the witch scenes from *Macbeth* — the world of literature that Bill knew and I didn't. He gave us a treasure box for literacy growth.

Bob Barton and I have included some effective poems for choral reading in our book *Poetry Goes to School*.

What kinds of poems are useful for choral reading?

As an example of oral and choral reading, dialogue poems are perfect scripts. Many of the poets writing for young people feature voices of all kinds. These "talking poems" can take different forms:

- monologues, in which the voice and the unseen audience provide sources for role-playing by the students;
- dialogues, which can serve as minimal scripts for the students to interpret in pairs, in small groups, or as a whole class divided into parts;
- question-and-answer poems in which students can explore the voices of those who may be speaking;
- chants, cheers, prayers, invocations, and songs, where students can raise their voices together as a village, a society, players in a game;
- situations so intense and concentrated that role-playing and improvisation present ways of discovering the voices within the poems

OVERHEARD ON A SALTMARSH

> Nymph, nymph, what are your beads?
> Green glass, goblin. Why do you stare at them?
> Give them me.
> No.
> Give them me. Give them me.
> No.
> Then I will howl all night in the reeds,
> Lie in the mud and howl for them.
> Goblin, why do you love them so?
> They are better than stars or water,
> Better than voices of winds that sing,
> Better than any man's fair daughter,
> Your green glass beads on a silver ring.
> Hush, I stole them out of the moon.
> Give me your beads, I desire them.
> No.
> I will howl in a deep lagoon
> For your green glass beads, I love them so.
> Give them me. Give them.
> No.

Harold Munro

This poem can lead to several activities involving choral reading:

- The students can work as partners, alternating the roles of Nymph and Goblin as they read the poem aloud several times.
- Partners can suggest and select a setting for their dramatization a marsh, a jungle, a cave, a playground.
- They can experiment with levels or space as they read, such as one partner standing and one lying down, exploring the reasons for the fight over the green glass beads.
- They can try whispering, shouting, or singing the lines.
- The whole class can read one part chorally, while the teacher or a student reads the other, and then the roles can be exchanged.

4

How can I organize an effective reading program?

What happens in a reading workshop?
How is it organized?

The answers to these questions will depend on other factors: your school schedules; preparation periods; revolving subject teachers; and so on. Some schools will have a literacy hour, while others will devote a morning to literacy, and include reading with technology as well. Still others will incorporate literacy events into their theme or inquiry time. For the reading workshop, I am suggesting three components: time for the whole class to explore literacy events together; group activity time for guided reading and novel study; and time for students to read independently with their own selected texts. You will have time constraints and opinions about how best to conduct these events, but I offer this structure as a point of organization, and you can fit the pieces into your own schedule. Of course, components such as time for individualized reading may take place even on subsequent days.

CLASS ACTITIVIES

During this community time, you can engage the students in a variety of activities:
- summarize the previous day's work;
- set the agenda for today's reading events;
- read aloud to the class: poems, folktales, and excerpts from novels;
- discuss the student responses you have finished reading, and read aloud responses by students that relate to issues under discussion;
- recognize general questions raised by the students;
- demonstrate and conduct mini-lessons on concerns or needs;
- present guest speakers or student panels;
- conduct a special drama session;
- involve the students in shared reading activities using charts, copies, or common texts and demonstrations.

Students can work in a variety of groupings throughout the year:
- in literature circles organized by theme, author, or genre;
- in guided reading groups in which explore how texts work;
- in group response activities;
- in sharing writing in reading journals.

INDEPENDENT OR INDIVIDUALIZED READING ACTIVITIES

On their own, students can:
- read books connected to literature circles;
- read books from the classroom library;
- participate in teacher conferences;
- write in reading journals;
- engage in any follow-up response to the text.

How should I use demonstrations and mini-lessons in my classroom?

How do I handle a literacy demonstration?

As we have seen, when we think out loud during the act of reading, we make the processing of ideas visible to our students, so that they see how we handle a piece of text either as a reader or as a writer. During these brief "think-aloud-and-show" sessions, we can reveal what we think before we read, while we read, and after we read. When students have opportunities to see our thinking processes in action, they may be able to apply similar strategies in their own work. If once a week you present a five-to-ten-minute demonstration of how you handle a text, within a year your students will have a repertoire of more than thirty types of texts that can reveal the different strategies proficient readers employ in making meaning.

With a grade-six class, I used two versions of the first Harry Potter novel, *Harry Potter and the Philosopher's* (*Sorcerer's* in the US) *Stone,* and compared lexical differences between the British and the American texts — *cooker* becomes *stove, sellotape* becomes *Scotch tape,* etc. (there are dozens and dozens of such changes) — and commented on the differences and which British expressions and words I would not have known. I said that I had decided that I personally would read the British versions, since England was the origin of the stories. The students had much to say after my demonstration of publishing mandates. I did mention that the next books in the series followed the British style. Cultural contexts matter in literacy.

What mini-lessons should I teach?

You can conduct a mini-lesson on one of the issues that has come up about reading or writing during reading or writing sessions. You can introduce a concept, present some examples, and ask the students to contribute and apply their understanding. These mini-lessons should be brief and concern one significant subject. Some possible mini-lessons include:
- differences between fiction and nonfiction books;

- characteristics of different genres;
- books written in the first, second, or third person;
- how authors use quotations;
- how the opening of a text can hook us;
- how authors use the problem/events/solution pattern in story structure;
- titles and their meanings;
- examples of foreshadowing;
- how authors use dialogue;
- predictable and surprise endings;
- how illustrations can enhance a story;
- secrets in books;
- asking questions while reading;
- making predictions in texts;
- using stick-it notes to mark interesting passages;
- looking for important ideas in texts.

How do I model literacy if I haven't read the books the students are reading?

The answer is to listen to them talk about their book, to engage in a conversation with them, to wonder about the text, to read the blurb on the back, to have them read to you their favourite passage, and then to read as many classroom books as possible. This was brought home to me teaching teachers in graduate programs. Of course they want to know what I am reading — the research, the articles, the books, the TED talks, the comments from guest speakers at conferences I attend. As teachers, we need to model our own literacy with our students as often as possible. We all remember teachers who read us a letter they had received, who read an editorial from a newspaper about an issue they cared deeply about, who showed us the novels they were reading or the information books they had found about their hobby. My high-school math teacher would try to solve the math puzzle in the morning newspaper each morning before our class began. He loved his discipline and told stories of its use in his pilot training during World War Two. I still remember him all these decades later.

Should students read independently during class time?

A few years ago, while working on a project using iPads with a seventh-grade all-boys class, I purchased multiple online copies of the novel *The Hunger Games*, first in a trilogy, which they read on their iPads for twenty minutes each day. After a week, the school got calls from several parents asking why their sons were asking for the next two books in the series. Shouldn't the school supply these? We couldn't keep up with their demands for more books; they had caught fire.

Students need to be encouraged to read at their own pace using materials they've chosen to read, in school time. We can give advice and help if asked, but the students need to decide what they will read. We can ensure that they make good choices by including a range of books in our class and in the school library. If students keep up-to-date records of the books they have read they can notice their reading patterns and widen the range if necessary. We need to represent a

In *This Is a Great Book*, Larry Swartz and Shelley Stagg Peterson present us with an excellent collection of titles of books for young people with which to build our classroom collections and our school libraries.

wide genre of books, including nonfiction, novels, folklore, poetry and picture books. While a few should be classics, most should be contemporary. Over time the students' concentration can be extended as can the level and range of reading material. Often we need to build atmosphere so that we can begin our program in the fall with uninterrupted and sustained silent reading time, and then gradually introduce conferences and community sharing.

I like to begin independent reading with a book talk featuring new additions to the classroom or school library, such as new books by favourite authors, books that I need to "sell" to the students because they are less familiar, books on relevant issues or media connections, or books representing different genres. We can talk about the issues involved in the story, connect the book to other books and issues. We can give a brief outline of the book, talk a bit about the plot or the characters, show the cover or illustrations, and offer our own personal response.

What are my choices in grouping students for reading instruction?

So that no student should feel locked in or out of a group for the whole year, we can implement a variety of flexible groupings and regroupings of students for different reading and writing events, so that their needs and interests can be met in a variety of teaching/learning situations, enabling students to move forward in their literacy development as they gain confidence and competence, and encouraging them to share their experiences with one another.

The process of creating and recreating effective groups is one that evolves as we become more familiar with our students. We need to observe and assess their abilities on an ongoing basis, and note the processes and strategies they are developing. We want to gather students together in groups that are flexible, groups in which they feel comfortable sharing their thoughts and reactions while working on specific strategies.

Debbie Diller presents such useful organizational strategies for implementing centres for group learning in her book *Literacy Work Stations*.

- We can form groups based on reading interests, activities, and topics students want to explore. Consider dividing your class into four large groups on a heterogeneous basis; within each group you can select a small group of students who need specific guidance. However, for many other activities, students will belong to the larger group so as not to feel segregated.
- For students who are just learning to read or who are having difficulty reading, we can group and regroup them for short periods during which, with peers who share similar reading problems, they can focus on an applicable topic or strategy.
- We can assess texts to determine if they meet the needs of the groups of students who will read them. There should be a variety of texts available to each group.
- We can often allow for students' preferences in forming groups, which can include working with friends, exploring a particular genre in depth, or studying the work of a specific author.
- I always have a brief check-in time with the whole class after group activities. I want the students to realize that I care about what happened in each group, that their actions were significant for them and for me.

What should happen in a reading conference?

A reading conference is an opportunity for you to have a conversation with a student or group of students about their reading, about the text, and the strategies and processes they are using. You may want to make quick notes to record your interactions; they might be as long as five minutes or as short as two minutes depending on the student and the purpose of the conference. You can teach on the spot one or two points that will support the student's success as a reader.

How we participate in conversations with a student or with a small group of students will often determine the success of our conferences. We need to engage them in a dialogue so that we can acquire information about them as readers and writers, and also decide whether we should offer specific help or just be supportive of their efforts and accomplishments. We need to confer with each of our students as frequently as possible, either with a brief check-in or an in-depth conference.

Years ago, Brian Crawford, a primary-school teacher enrolled in a doctoral program, wrote his thesis about his method of conferring with his students: during recess, he would spend five minutes chatting with one student at a time about their reading progress, the books they were enjoying, the ideas of group members, or the stories he had shared with them in circle time. I have kept a copy of his thesis to remind me of how truly professional teachers structure their events for maximum success.

How does "text talk" support comprehension?

What seems to help readers in developing a deeper, more fully realized understanding of a text is to share personal meanings and responses with others by participating in discussions with classmates and the teacher in literature circles, book clubs, reading groups, or conferences. By going public with their responses, they increase the connections they can make with those who are reading alongside them. Individual responses are both shared and altered by the contributions of the participants, and often by the nurturing support of the teacher.

Talk is the optimal comprehension strategy. We frame our literature journeys as inquiries, participating in the quest for increasing our understanding by making connections with what others are thinking out loud as they grope and stumble towards meaning. We surprise each other into knowing. We learn to hold our ideas tentatively, to invite our partners in conversation into our uncertain forest of ideas. It is the dynamic of the interplay among members of the literacy community that enables and engenders the processes of meaning-making. In school, our strength as educators lies in the interactions we establish among the students, where they learn from and because of each other, in socially constructed discourse. As true conversation among student discussants twists and turns, everyone is engaged in the act of building understanding. We are having literary conversations, and expanding our comprehension by leaps and bounds.

How do literature circles work?

Literature circles, book clubs, or novel groups are mixed groups of students formed on the basis of the same book choices. Each group should meet two or three times a week in order to carry on a continuing conversation about their

Revisiting Harvey Daniels's book *Literature Circles, 2nd Edition* continues to help me refine my own strategies for working with novels in book club groupings.

books. They will need to decide on how much should be read before each session — what I call checkpoints — and if they read ahead, group members should reread the portion that will be discussed. In-depth discussions will be supported by the notes, comments, and drawings the group members have prepared in their reading journals while involved with their reading of the text.

Everyone should be encouraged to participate, supporting each other's comments, moving the discussion along, and helping to keep the talk focused on the ideas generated by the text. Through these conversations, readers learn to support their ideas with references to the texts, to pose questions that have real significance, and to accept or at least consider the opinions of others when they disagree. They will be involved in thinking and reading about the text in a collaborative activity as they interact with others, learning about themselves as they deepen and expand their meaning-making.

It may help to provide a group with some suggestions for the discussion about their book as they read through it. Some teachers organize a pre-reading session about the books with their groups — the cultural references, the time in which the story takes place, and so on. Will the class read the text chapter by chapter, or in sections followed by book talk? Some teachers assign roles for group members, change them when necessary, and discard them as the students become trained in how to engage in rich conversations. I think bringing something new to the table can stimulate talk and encourage a wider response to what has been read and said. You could ask a student volunteer to assume one role for each discussion time, so that the group feels enriched and engaged by the support that is offered by the student leader. For instance:

- An instigator can raise issues drawn from the previous group reading (some suggested questions from a classroom resource chart may help).
- A linguist can note the specific language and structures used in the section (slang, dialect, expressions, etc.).
- An art curator can bring information about the cover art of a book, or download pictures representing the theme, the time, the place, the issues of the story, etc.
- A reteller can summarize previously read sections (perhaps in role as a character in the book).
- A critic, at the close of the novel, can offer commentary about the author and reviews of the book, using Internet resources.

Sometimes I am a silent participant, observing and gathering information concerning the students' reading behaviours, their group dynamics, their comprehension strategies. Other times, I can model and demonstrate effective ways to contribute to a discussion. I can act as a facilitator, making positive comments that support and affirm the contributions of the students, encouraging them to refer to the text to provide evidence for their ideas, and moving them toward analyzing and synthesizing their thoughts as they move along in the conversation.

And there will be times when I need to intervene directly about problems they are having with the text, pointing out information they have missed, or clarifying a complex issue. I can restate a point for emphasis, synthesize the ideas they have presented, or extend the direction of their thinking on an issue. But my teaching/learning goal has to be to guide the group's growing ability to monitor their own progress, so that they can take charge of their learning and move themselves into a deeper and more meaningful discussion.

A few moments for guided reflection, oral or written, at the conclusion of each session will help the students assess their own contributions and the quality of the group's participation. They can share comments, questions, and insights and make decisions about the direction the next meeting should take, such as clarifying their roles to strengthen subsequent discussions. A quick self-assessment sheet might look like this:

SELF-ASSESSMENT:			
	Yes	No	Sometimes
I was prepared for today's reading.			
I made contributions to the group's discussion.			
I listened to my group members.			
I asked questions about the book.			
I shared my opinion about the book.			
I referred to the book to support my point of view.			
I helped the group solve problems.			
I was able to retell parts of the story.			
I commented on the author's style and use of language.			
I developed a better understanding of the book because of the literature circle.			
My strengths in the literature circle included:			
Areas I still need to work on include:			
My most valuable contribution to the group today was:			
Our discussion helped me understand this book in these ways:			
These topics were still not clear to me after we finished our discussion:			

Irene Fountas and Gay Su Pinnell include a wealth of useful suggestions in their books for teachers. I still refer to *Guiding Readers and Writers* in constructing my own ideas for instructional reading groups.

Audio-recording a group's book talk can offer a powerful demonstration of the kinds of text talk the students are engaged in. As well, sections of the dialogue — critical moments in the discussion — can be transcribed by the teacher or preferably by a group of students who choose from the recorded conversations "memorable moments of dialogue" to share with the class.

How should I use guided reading?

This is an important question in today's literacy classrooms. Some teachers are worried about guided reading times: they may seem artificial and teacher-directed. But to me they resemble book clubs or literature circles, except the goal is different: we want students to explore a shared text in order to develop a particular understanding of how print works, how one form of text functions, and how they can become more proficient as readers by coming to understand the workings of print with a text they can handle at their reading stage. Because the text is accessible, the students can take this opportunity to examine it; we can draw attention to story structures and significant graphics and illustrations, and support readers who are attempting unfamiliar words, helping them to apply their word-solving phonic skills to identify them and solve them quickly. They can practice their self-monitoring skills and become more independent as readers. Students are guided and supported in applying their knowledge of how readers function, attending to the story content, the text structure, and the words.

A critical aspect of the guided reading process is to match books to individual students. To accomplish this goal with efficiency, it is necessary to organize the books so that the teacher's decisions can be faster, easier, and more effective. Texts for instruction or guided reading sessions can be organized in a variety of ways. The most important consideration in assigning a level to a book rests on whether students at the level can read at a rate of 90–95-percent accuracy. For each level, there should be several books. We can group students whose abilities, knowledge, and experience are similar. Multiple copies of books for a group instruction session in the primary grades can help set the stage for young readers to achieve the skills they will require in becoming independent readers. Text formats, text features, text mediums, along with quality of literature and interests and backgrounds of the reader — all factor into leveling texts for the individual. If I were working with students having difficulties accessing print, I would want to use leveled texts for my instructional time with them, and open their choices during independent and inquiry times. There are countless guides and lists of leveled books available in print and online, such as the *National Geographic Readers*, Scholastic's *Little Leveled Readers,* or Rubicon's *Boldprint Kids.*

> Young readers need texts at appropriate levels. Leveled text is a useful teaching tool for guided reading, as long as it is used in the classroom as one part of a balanced reading program that includes shared reading and read-aloud experiences. When teachers use leveled texts, it should be to support and scaffold students' learning in guided reading instruction and as a part of independent reading.
>
> Shelley Stagg Peterson,
>
> *Why Leveled Books Have a Specific and Limited Role in Teaching Reading*

KEY COMPONENTS OF A GUIDED READING SESSION

- Group students who share a similar reading level.
- Choose an appropriate text for the group that will lead to reading success.
- Ask the students to sit in a circle.
- Introduce the text by looking at accompanying pictures (especially with emergent readers), and discuss a few potentially difficult words, the concepts, and the purpose of reading.

- Ask students to read the text silently, if possible, and independently.
- Observe them as they read the text. Make notes of your observations.
- At the end of the reading, discuss the text with students — its plot, vocabulary, and concepts, and especially the reading strategies they used. Students can then take part in an extension activity, such as talking as if they were characters, or drawing the setting of the story.
- Focus on rereading parts of the text as necessary for the discussion.
- Draw attention to word patterns and sentence patterns to help in identifying unfamiliar words.
- Complete a running record with one student per group.
- Assess the students' development. Note those who need to move to another group.

How do I know if a book is at the right reading level for the student? What if a student chooses to read books that are too easy? What if a student chooses to read books that are too hard?

Many years ago I watched a fifth-grade boy work his laboured way through *Tom Sawyer* because his dad had said it was a great book. He finished it and felt very successful. Today, I have support strategies to help him; I might even suggest a different title. But his pride in finishing his dad's choice says he was right.

Leveled books are best used during instructional times, such as guided reading, when the teacher can suggest appropriate texts for the students at their approximate stages of reading success. Whether a text is easy or hard for a child depends on more than the characteristics inherent in the text. The way the text is introduced and supportive interaction during reading play important roles as well. We teachers need to continuously balance the possible tension between text level and the amount of support we can provide to readers. We need to know how individual students approach texts since that knowledge allows us to provide appropriate resources. If students are selecting books during independent reading time that are not challenging enough, it may be that they want to revisit an author or a topic, they want to be participants in a popular series, or they are lacking enough support in choosing books. If the latter is true I like to make a suggestion: "Here are three books for you to choose from; which one do you think is best for you?"

Of course, classroom resources include all types of texts and text forms, and students will have opportunities to:
- work with instructional leveled texts;
- find self-selected materials during independent reading;
- search online materials during inquiry projects;
- reread a book for a sense of comfort and success;
- be included in reading a popular text with their buddies by having a talking book.

What are the signs of a struggling reader?

Which of the following descriptors seem to match the struggling students in your classroom, or do students demonstrate combinations of behaviours, attitudes, and abilities at different times and in different literacy situations with different kinds of texts? Struggling readers may:

- not be involved in family literacy and seem unfamiliar with literature;
- not read fluently, either silently or orally;
- lack faith and confidence that they will learn to be effective readers and writers;
- demonstrate frustration or apathy during reading times because of previous failure and humiliation;
- fail to understand why reading can be worthwhile;
- not see books and other print resources as sources of pleasure and information;
- avoid reading at every opportunity;
- not know the alphabet, or not understand how print works in a text;
- feel that reading is only the correct recognition and pronunciation of words;
- not know basic rimes and sound/symbol patterns;
- be unable to process new words as they read, and seldom reread to self-check and correct miscues;
- have few strategies for dealing with unfamiliar words, and over-rely on sounding out;
- have difficulty matching their story-memory predictions with the actual print words;
- be unable to recognize high-frequency words while reading;
- ignore punctuation that could increase comprehension;
- rely constantly upon the teacher for support in decoding and encoding words;
- be unable to hold the parts of complex sentences in their minds to build the larger text meaning, relying on poor substitutions and lacking background vocabulary or content information;
- not understand how a reader reads silently, and when they attempt to read silently claim that their mind wanders;
- be afraid to take risks in order to construct meaning;
- be unable to bring personal background information to meaning-making with a particular text;
- focus on literal interpretation of text instead of inferring, analyzing, synthesizing, and extending the reading;
- not monitor whether the reading experience makes sense (never say, "Hey! That doesn't make sense!");
- be unable to predict future events in the text, the force that drives us to continue reading;
- falter frequently while reading aloud, often pleading (even silently) for help;
- be unable to retell a text;
- be defeated by the length of the text;
- be unable to select a book or choose inappropriate books for their interests and abilities.

How do I help students in reading difficulty?

Just as non-swimmers are given opportunities outside of instruction time to play in the pool, students need to experience what successful literacy events feel like, to know that there is hope for recovery, that they will be supported in their struggle to grow toward independence. They need to become real readers and writers with texts they can handle. Very few students are unable to master literacy; we will need to recognize and help many different types of struggling readers and writers, to find out what they can do and build on their competencies, no matter how limited, so that they can move forward and recognize that they are indeed improving. They will want to make choices in their literacy lives, to sense ownership of their reading and writing selves, by selecting some of the books they read, the topics they write about, and the projects they research. They will care more about activities they feel they own, in which they will want to invest their time and interest.

When these youngsters are not isolated but find themselves sometimes sitting alongside others in the classroom literacy community who are involved in and excited about learning, they have role models for what life in school could be. They can begin to sense how readers and writers function. I have seen older students become buddy readers with younger students, and watched as they began to see themselves as those who can read, who have power with print. There will be occasions when you want to work with a small group of students who are having difficulties, but for the rest of the day, it's important to make literacy events social and communicative experiences in which readers of mixed abilities are interacting with satisfaction alongside their companions.

You may need to help these students set short-term goals or break a complex task into smaller steps. They will need brief but regular conferences and checkpoints, in order for you to offer support and provide direction that will move them ahead toward success. This will be especially true while working in the content areas, both with what they must read and with follow-up activities. Literacy development can occur with all text experiences, not just in reading and writing workshops.

Once when I was introducing online texts to an all-boys grade-seven class, we were reading a short story on their iPads. I was checking who had finished when one student said, "Mr. Booth, I don't think Brandon has found the story." Two boys then turned to help him with his problem, and we went on discussing the qualities of heroes. Brandon took his time completing his reading, and the other two boys stayed beside him monitoring and helping. This struggling reader had discovered iPad Power. By the way, those were the most caring boys, looking after each other, that I have met in a long time. Their teacher had clearly nurtured a sense of community in the classroom that made learning richer — and easier — for all the students.

RELUCTANT READERS

Reluctant readers are students who can read but for whatever reason don't choose to. We cannot group all reluctant readers together, for there are many different reasons for their difficulties, many stumbling blocks to their growing as readers: their background experiences; how they feel about themselves as learners; their interests in the context of the classroom (the teacher's skills and attitudes, the resources, the pressures of curriculum). We can stress cooperative learning activities, where students read and write with a partner or small group about literature, mathematics, scientific reports, or historical documents. And we can use books that have strong appeal and accessible reading levels. We can give them choice in selecting texts and topics for research, and create opportunities for them to feel that their work matters to others through sharing their findings with the class, and giving them leadership roles in organizing inquiries.

Two boys in grade six were completing an inquiry into mining. They had chosen to research the dangers of working underground and felt they were finished after finding one newspaper article. In our discussions, I mentioned all of the materials our society uses which ultimately come from underground resources. The boys were unaware of many of these materials, and I asked them to explore how we would cope in the absence of the materials that are now mined. They turned to their laptops and worked for three days, first listing the items, then researching if there were substitutes for them, and finally locating data on robots as miners. Gradually their focus changed to issues of replacement of human labour, and after their presentation, I asked them what jobs there might now be for unemployed miners. Always more to read, write, and discover.

Why do some students give up when asked to read a text on their own?

Non-readers, unmotivated readers, reluctant readers, limited readers, can all change with the right set of conditions. We hear stories from those who work with adult illiterates about how their students eventually and with support come to be stronger with print texts. We hear from teachers who work with youngsters in remedial reading classes of the great strides many of them make from guidance and instruction. And we listen to the stories of those who struggled with reading, some of them teachers and writers, who, with the help of someone who understood the reading process, gained membership in the literacy club.

These are some signs of reading breakdown that we can help our students to notice and to modify:

There are too many hard words in the selection, and I am giving up.
Generally speaking, if there are more than five difficult words on a page that the reader can't readily solve, the text is too difficult. Readers need to find a simpler version, or to do some pre-work with the ideas, the words, or the structure of the text. It seldom helps to look up a number of words in a dictionary before reading, but finding information on one or two important terms may help the reader to understand other words in context. Often a discussion before reading can present the students with enough background and terminology to make meaning with the words. Of course, efficient readers know to omit a difficult word or to flag it until they have read further and have more information to bring to recognizing it.

I can't remember what I am reading about.
If a reader can't retell part of what has just been read, then he/she has to go back and take stock of the text, review the purpose for reading, do some more pre-work on the text, or reread what has gone before. There is little sense in continuing when they have lost their way. They need to stop and retell what they remember so far, or consider what has happened.

I don't care what I am reading about.
The reader has lost the purpose for reading the selection. There is no interaction with the author or the text. Instead of questioning the ideas on the page, arguing or wondering about the content, the reader has stopped interacting with the print. It might be useful for the reader to begin predicting what could happen next, and then rethink and revise their guesses as they find out more information.

I'm thinking about something unconnected to the text.

All readers shift back and forth between the print and other ideas unrelated to the text. But the proficient reader recognizes this wandering and attempts to connect with the ideas in the text by connecting it with events in life.

I'm not finding answers to the questions that I ask as I read the text.

The reader needs more background or clarification about the text before the meanings can build. If our questions begin to pile up as we read, we need to step back from the text and find a stronger orientation to what we are reading. Good readers learn to preview the text they are about to read, to notice its organizational structure, its format, how it fits in with their past reading and life experiences. In that sense, they can read what they already know.

I can't create any visual images from the text.

If the reader can't make any pictures from the words in the text, then meaning has been interrupted, and the mind is not imagining what the words are creating. It takes practice to paint mental pictures from the text, but as the reader becomes more adept, the ideas in the text grow clearer, and new connections can be made with the reader's background experiences. Slowing down is a good way to enable more reflection and visualization.

I read it but I have no idea what it was about.

By using some of the strategies they have explored during the year, students could become aware of their difficulties as they reread and work towards handling the confusion. Should they highlight information that puzzles them? Do they need to jot down questions that arise as they read? Should they reread the introduction or the blurb on the back cover of a book? Do they need to check a difficult term in the glossary? Do they need a brief conference with the teacher to get them back on track? Can they begin to make connections with the text as they read, relating other background experiences, both in print and in life, to this text?

I'm afraid to recognize that I can't understand what I am reading.

By ignoring or disguising confusion or a breakdown in their reading, or by not monitoring the problems with meaning-making with a text, students can't make decisions about their comprehension problems and strengths, and can't learn how to bring themselves back to making sense of their reading. The first step towards a solution is isolating the difficulty and selecting a strategy that can help. Sometimes writing down a response or a summary of what has been learned so far helps clarify the direction the text is taking.

I never skim or scan to find main ideas or important facts; I never adjust my reading rate.

Often we need to scan the text to get the gist of it before we read a specific passage, or skim a page to find the point that connects to what we have just read. Readers need to understand the structure of text, to note any features that might help in understanding — captions, marginalia, summaries, etc. — and then bring that information back to their reading. Onscreen texts offer excellent practice in skimming and scanning.

How can I encourage extensive reading rather than focusing on one book for months?

In my own work in the teaching of reading strategies, I am seldom satisfied unless the learning stretches outside the classroom lives of the students, connecting their reading to the bigger world so that their customary perspectives and assumptions are challenged or altered.

This question offers us opportunities for promoting extensive reading, where students explore a variety of texts on an issue or a theme. The Internet can expand the extent of the reading resources, so that students can find different versions, new information, narratives, interviews, videos, and begin to build an awareness of not only the topic, but the process of researching, of reviewing, of checking reliable sources.

For example, when students experience two or more stories that are related in some way, their understanding of each is altered and enriched by the other, as they make connections between their expanding lives and the stories. Often one text prepares the reader for another one, facilitating the understanding of the subsequent story. And, of course, each new story sheds light on past story experiences, creating a changing view of the stories in the student's story repertoire. Students can meet all kinds of different texts in a book set, and then focus on similarities and differences; individuals can each read a different story, and then share their understandings and findings. As teachers, we also add our own selections, some to be read or told aloud, others to be left on a table to be read by volunteers. One story gives birth to a thousand.

While working on a project with one theme, the Selchies (half-seal, half-human), I discovered so many stories, films, and poems about this folklore, a comprehensive book set. Each version has its own dynamics, its particular way of framing how we create meaning with the telling. I shared different versions with some classes, and a single telling with others. How each group of students made literacy sense of these stories formed my book *Exploding the Reading*. The different stories and versions included:

1. *The Seal Mother* by Mordicai Gerstein
2. *The Boy who Lived with Seals (an Aboriginal Tale)* by Rafe Martin
3. *The Selchie Girl* by Susan Cooper
4. *Greyling* by Jane Yolen
5. *Seal Song* by Andrea Spalding
6. *Una and the Sea Cloak* by Malachy Doyle
7. *Poems of Magic and Spells* edited by William Cole
8. *Neptune Rising* by Jane Yolen
9. *The Norse Myths* by Kevin Crossley-Holland
10. *The Crane Wife* by Katherine Paterson
11. "The Great Silkie of Sule Skerry" (folksong)
12. "One Spared to the Sea" (a traditional folktale)
13. "Kopakonan, the Seal-Woman" (folktale)
14. "Ballad of the White Seal Maid" (folksong)
15. *The Selchie's Midnight Song* by Jane Yolen

How do I help students move beyond "pop culture" in their reading and viewing?

A couple of years ago, my granddaughter enjoyed singing the theme song from *Frozen* to me on the phone. Now for her it is a relic from the past. We shouldn't trivialize or mock children's choices at different stages of their literacy careers. We know that we read the same book or view the same film (never mind the hit songs) through different eyes as we grow into our lives, and often we are shocked at our new response to a text we thought we knew with our hearts and minds. As I mentioned earlier, I reread *Black Beauty* as an adult with a class of grade-six students only to find it is about an anthropomorphic talking horse who represents the class structure of England from a hundred years ago. The students and I were now involved in reading a very different book from the one I had discovered some fifty years before.

Across time, my accumulated experiences from my research and reading and relationships have altered my responses and reactions to every text I meet — media texts, print texts, people texts. My world of understanding has exploded. Similarly, students construct their meanings with a book or a film from the viewpoint of their own developing experiences. Where they have been will determine where they go with a text. Eve Merriam said, "It takes a lot of slow to grow."

As teachers, we have all experienced the disappointment that comes from a student revealing his boredom or dissatisfaction with what we had felt was a wonderful piece of literature. It is a complicated task finding appropriate and interesting books (online and on the page) that represent quality literature for our students, but we do want them to be "extending the boundary of their own knowing," as Maryann Eeds and Ralph Peterson put it in *Grand Conversations: Literature Groups in Action*. If only they would enjoy what we told them to enjoy, or like a book because we said they should. Backgrounds and abilities differ widely in the ages and stages of their school years, and we need to value the variety of texts that can and might help them grow.

I've had my share of failed attempts to broaden students' reading. Douglas, a boy in my grade-five class, always chose books on science for his individual reading. I asked the librarian to assist him in making wider choices, hoping to enlarge his background in both genre and literature, but we failed. He continued to make this his field of interest, and as it turned out he eventually became a scientist. Still, I would want our scientists to be aware of how people live emotionally, socially, and collectively, and literature can help. My bias is too strong; I personally read all kinds of texts, choose a film to fit my mood, laugh when my granddaughter reads me a simple series book. Reading, viewing, listening are usually context-dependent. Especially for me. In my world Elvis is alive! In my granddaughter's he doesn't exist.

Should older students work with younger classes?

In my dream school, this kind of work would be mandatory. I am not sure who learns most: the younger students or the older students, or perhaps the two teachers who then have much-needed time to observe the two groups and note age and stage patterns. It really is based on a big brother/big sister model, and is one of the best strategies for reducing bullying that I have found.

In one high school, I had been invited to work with a class of drama students. Fortunately, there was a primary school across the playground, and those young students could present a perfect audience for a low-threat sharing of the secondary students' work. We spent most of the class exploring information researched on the Internet about the habits and behaviours of coyotes, and then built stories — myths — about an imagined coyote culture, weaving the data into first-person lore that could be shared.

For the last ten minutes, we all crossed the playground to the primary school, and I asked the secondary coyote people to wait in the hall. The primary teacher had read a story about farmers troubled by coyotes, and the students as reporters had developed questions they would like to ask the farmers and coyote people.

I then instructed the primary students to lie on the floor as journalists, tired from interviewing and writing about the farmers and their problems. They were to close their eyes and dream about the coyotes. In the silence of the room, the high-school students crept in and, one on one, whispered their mythic stories in the ears of the students lying quietly on the floor. When they were finished, these older students crept away, and I asked the young students as journalists to wake and open their eyes. Perhaps their responses were the most fascinating of all the dramas I have been involved in. The primary students spoke as if they had indeed dreamed the entire visit:

"I think I had a dream and went to coyote land where they told me stories."

"This coyote told me about how he hunted and found food, and I think I was with him while he hunted."

"My coyote said that we were special and we could help them live and I heard her and I want to tell the farmers."

The stories went on and on, and I am not sure if the students were able to separate the drama and the dreams, but when I reflected later with the secondary students, they felt excited about the sharing of their explorations. This had become an unusual and powerful moment in the lives of both the high-school and primary students.

In a previous section I mentioned buddy reading, and this type of collaboration provides opportunities for deep interactions between classes. Even taking an second-grade class to work alongside a sixth-grade class can change the behaviours of all concerned. Our strong community is strengthened by our time with other strong communities; we grow together.

How can I promote effective reading in the content subjects?

Texts and Lessons for Content-Area Reading by Harvey Daniels and Nancy Steineke contains dozens of different and unusual out-of-school texts for demonstrating literacy strategies.

I remember visiting a school where the principal had organized a large science room for the fourth-, fifth-, and sixth-grade students. He told me that he felt his school-wide literacy program was weak, yet he had an amazing science teacher. Each class visited the science room for an hour three times a week, and I saw more literacy activity in that room than I have seen in many language arts rooms. The program was planned with exceeding care: starting a new theme each week, the students signed up for and worked in small groups at established centres, well supplied with all types of resources. They had to follow assignment cards at each work station and present their findings at the end of the third period. The room was always buzzing, and everyone was working. The teacher monitored and assisted where necessary, and group roles were assigned. The expectations were high, and I witnessed collaborative behaviours everywhere. There are times when planning and organization encourage and increase literacy growth, in every subject. This was one excellent example.

Why is nonfiction the main focus of so many school literacy programs?

Over time, students are expected to read independently and more frequently, to read longer and more difficult texts in a variety of curriculum areas, to read faster and more selectively, to remember more information, and to make integrative connections. They also have to learn new words and terms in all their different subjects. Often, we educators forget the difficulties inherent in using a single textbook for mathematics or science, or the complexities involved in reading information books or information online. Schools have begun to recognize the importance of reading across the curriculum, mainly nonfiction, and technology has opened a great deal of information and other types of nonfiction texts. Teachers can play a valuable role in helping students notice text features in different genres, giving them much-needed access to those texts.

Students need a purpose for reading what we assign in every subject. They need to know how to focus on the reading process, what they will be expected to do with what they find when they are finished, and how to handle the type of text they are required to read — instructions, letters, narratives, or information, online and on page. If the text seems unfamiliar, or disconnected from their previous understanding of the issue, if it's full of different words or terms, then we need to help them find ways to handle what they are required to understand. They need a reading roadmap to know how effective readers read complicated texts; they need at times to read as scientists, sociologists, mathematicians, and artists, depending upon the texts. Different text expectations require different strategies, forms, and formats. For example: How do we take notes when we conduct an experiment? How will we then summarize what has happened? How can we take time to work with our students in handling a lengthy, complicated science text?

One grade-eight class examined six tables of contents that I had gathered from six different history textbooks, to make some connections about how the books appeared to be structured, why the information had been arranged in a particular way, and the intent of each author team that could be deduced from these opening pages. It became a literacy adventure, and we used their discoveries throughout the year with our own textbook, as a guide for understanding how those authors attempted to make sense of history. The students were connecting their text with how other texts were designed and formatted. I only wish they could as an informed class have chosen the book for the year that they had decided appeared most appropriate, but we did make use of the other five books they had examined in groups.

PROMPTS FOR READING INFORMATION TEXTS

How is information organized (by topic, in time, by contrasting ideas, etc.)? Does the total format of the text help you understand the topic better? What does the title tell you about this text? What genre does the selection represent? How is this book like other books you've read in this genre? How do headings and subheadings help you find information in this text? What did you learn about this topic? Were you reminded of anything in your own life? What does this book make you think or wonder about? What surprised you? How does the information in this text fit with what you already know? Why did the author think this subject was important? If you were the author, would you change the order of any of the material? What information is provided through illustrations (drawings, diagrams, maps, charts, etc.)? Would you read other books by this author?

How can I best facilitate a home reading program?

Parents as educational partners

When I began teaching, my principal told me to cover the window in the door with some paper, so that parents waiting in the hall couldn't see in. Now schools want to develop realistic collaborative goals for working alongside parents. By listening to parents, we can discover a great deal about family literacy in their homes and incorporate that knowledge into the programs we develop for their kids. We can increase communication through interviews or phone calls, via a secure blog, or in a classroom newsletter, so that they are aware of how our program functions and can give appropriate support. We can discuss how to assist a troubled reader, why a child needs to read a book silently before sharing it aloud, how to chat with a child about their reading and writing, how to find a quiet time for reading, how to extend the range of literacy events in the family setting with TV guides or by writing weekly menus, how to use the classroom and public libraries to locate books to read aloud (perhaps with a babysitter or older sibling).

Recently I participated in a webinar for the Durham Catholic Parent Involvement Committee; two hundred parents tuned in online to presentations by the literacy consultant and me. These parent committees are vital for bringing school policies and parents' concerns together, and throughout the evening the parents sent emails in to us with their questions, stimulating honest conversation about the literacy education of their children. We need more involving activities such as this one with parents, so that our literacy challenges can be handled together; home and school together have the power to change education.

I am possibly more frustrated by homework policies than by any other aspect of school. We need to involve parents wherever possible, without adding guilt or stress to their lives, in all aspects of their kids' literacy progress, while remembering that they are not teachers, and that reading and writing experiences at home should be natural and positive so that children can be helped to work through their difficulties, not punished for failing to do so. Homework is often a troubling time for students and parents; we need to be aware of the demands we place on students, offer parents specific and clear suggestions to help them understand what needs to be achieved each night, and explain how those tasks will support the children's growth as readers and writers. We need to value parents as partners in the education of students. Too many parents are concerned about the amount of time their children are spending on homework assignments. Schools need to develop a fair policy concerning homework that truly benefits their children.

In my opinion, any books sent home in primary grades to be read aloud to parents have to be carefully monitored, or both parent and child will find reading their books a chore, not a worthwhile experience. One school asked me about requiring reading journals to be completed every night after reading. This is a common practice but it seems excessive to me. If an activity creates negative learning, we should modify or even stop it. A school community can find a different and better way of promoting independent reading. Most reading should be done in class, where there are teachers trained and prepared to help a child move towards literacy proficiency. Reading may need to be accomplished in bite-sized chunks, each evening, so the pattern is established, but it needs to be achievable in a two-bedroom apartment with three children around the kitchen table, with two parents who have worked hard all day, with time for a scout meeting, hockey practice, and some screen time. Learning how to accomplish school tasks at home is useful, but only if the task can be accomplished without the teacher.

In my son's home, traditional homework is done after school, but he plays board games with his two children most evenings after dinner. They are complicated games, often in three dimensions (they have over fifty games to choose from), and the children are learning so much from these literacy experiences. Mara, eight, checks the instructions manual at almost every throw of the dice or spin of the wheel. Elijah, six, handles his own cards and has acquired an amazing sight-word vocabulary. I would eliminate the gaming part of the evening if I were in charge. Fortunately I am not: this is one case where the parents are teaching something I can't.

5

Is writing a period in the school day or part of every subject?

Should writing instruction happen, for example, in science and social studies?

Writing is writing, no matter the curriculum subject, the topic, or the reason for writing. Effective teachers explain how each function of writing works in each genre, from taking notes to brainstorming a list for an issue involving social justice to developing a collaborative picture book. The style for each genre or form follows the function for which we are writing. We now know that there are many things to teach about reading and writing through instructional mini-lessons, demonstrations, or conferences in all subjects. We learn to write as scientists and historians and mathematicians. But I know that for me, acquiring the bits and pieces of the writer's craft requires as much time as it takes the cabinetmaker to learn how to handle different kinds of wood; mentoring, mistakes, and reflection will be part of the learning. We can make great use of writing time when we look at the craft required for each genre, when we observe mentor texts that give us patterns and suggestions for how we can arrange our thoughts and information, when we can explore ways for revising, editing, and sharing our work. Technology often requires support in order for students to use these tools effectively. Learning to communicate through writing is a cumulative, lifelong process. We can only help our young writers with what they can achieve at this moment in their writing lives. I use writers' workshops in my own class. Writing is itself a kind of reading, and the reader should be considering the writer as he/she reads, asking questions, predicting. Students need to write several times each day, for different reasons, in different genres, and for shared experiences with others who read their written work. Some types of written communication:

- messagerie: the process of using messages, social media, correspondence;
- free writing: spontaneous, unjudged, brainstorming, journals;
- records: minutes, surveys, study notes, jottings;
- reportage: essays, PowerPoint, inquiries;
- poetry: forms, styles, free verse, rhythm and rhyme;

- scripts: PowerPoint, films, tableaux, presentations, YouTube videos;
- procedures: science experiments, computer games;
- opinions: reviews, columns;
- narratives: life stories, biographies;
- descriptions: settings, landmarks, images in words.

What happens in a writing workshop?

In a writing community, each member's work is considered significant, and feedback and dialogue are needed and valued. Rather than having students view their writing as an assignment to be finished as quickly as possible, the writing workshop, when used as a regular classroom routine, can help them recognize the significance of generating meaningful topics and the need to revise and edit as they move toward final drafts. Students become more proficient by writing at regularly scheduled times for authentic purposes — real reasons for behaving as writers. They come to know their own developing abilities, what needs to be worked on and what can be celebrated.

- You can begin a writing workshop with a brief talk about writing, using examples from picture books, novel excerpts, biographies of writers, or your own life's writing. Teachers need to share their own stories with students and encourage them to author their life histories as readers and writers. As well, teachers need to use their own writing as a model, sharing copies of notes and memos, demonstrating a writing event (such as creating a parent newsletter), showing that writing remains a significant aspect of adult life. Students need to see teachers revising, struggling, crossing out, adding and moving text, referencing and publishing.

- This can be followed by a mini-lesson related to the aspects of writing you want the students to understand, or those drawn from your observations of student needs. You should focus on aspects of writing that the students can apply to their own writing. Students can take notes in their writing notebooks for future reference. For example, students can participate in an interactive editing session with a sample of work you copy onto a shared screen. The students can alter the text in a variety of ways — combining sentences, choosing alternate words, spelling, noticing attributes of words.

- Students usually write independently for half an hour or more while you confer with individuals or small groups to offer guidance and feedback. During independent writing, students are engaged at different times in a variety of activities, but they will either be writing or working on some aspect of the writing process — focusing on a topic in their notebook, working in a small-group peer sharing, revising their structure, using resources and references, editing for accurate use of conventions, preparing for publication or conferring with the teacher. Students can choose a project they would like to work on and decide if they want to work alone, with a partner, or as part of a small group. Students should write silently and move around only when necessary. Conferences can be conducted in quiet conversational tones.

We can continue to take time to respond to their writing, on paper and electronically, as we encourage them to develop and expand their jottings and recollections. By doing so, we can redirect their reading, suggest new books, share our own writing journey, and elaborate upon their thoughts, so that they will be stimulated to continue their writing about reading.

We can continue to help the students acquire handwriting skills that promote an easy flow of ideas and support communication with others. Students often are defeated by the mechanics of creating written text. Authorities such as Donald Graves tell us that continuous authentic writing through the years will support handwriting improvement, and that maturity will have an effect on how we form our words. My own son represents this growth so very clearly: by grade seven and eight, his troubled handwriting had become so small it was almost unreadable, but he was rescued by the computer, and his handwriting became legible and uniform because his confidence as a communicator had blossomed.

What should students write about?

International educator Gordon Wells has taught me so much about the functions of writing in our lives. In his book *Dialogic Inquiry*, he offers four basic requirements for our programs:

1. The writing projects the students are engaged in must have significance for the other members of their community.
   (We want to participate in these literacy events. Our classroom community recognizes that we need to write as a life process.)
2. The topic needs to be of interest to the writer, who must believe that there is more to discover about it.
   (I want to write about this topic; it continues to interest me. There is something more out there in the world to discover than what I know right now.)
3. The writer needs to care enough about the aesthetic quality of the writing so that he/she will attempt to solve problems that arise in the process of creating it.
   (I want to revise my work for you; it matters. I want you the reader to have access to my thoughts, my information and my feelings, and to notice how I have ordered and arranged them.)
4. The writer must be able to count on members of the community to provide support and resources when he/she feels it to be necessary.
   (I want you to help me grow as a writer when I ask you, and I will support you in your efforts as well.)

We need to develop authentic reasons for having boys and girls write, so they will value opportunities for writing for a variety of functions and for different audiences. We need to help students find reasons and methods for revising and editing their written work, and then offer them ways of sharing the final drafts.

We need to create time for students to spend in writing, actually composing and arranging their ideas. For many, talking about what they may write is a prerequisite for the process of writing, so that they are prepared and confident when they begin to compose their thoughts. Webs, lists, brainstormed ideas, and, of course, computers can help them move immediately into the act of writing instead of worrying and stalling for time. They can begin to take charge of their revision and editing, reading their work aloud to themselves and noting incongruities, using computer spell checks and other reference resources. We need to let the students in on the secrets of writing.

Teachers using the inquiry model, with students working individually or in groups, will need to offer support in the various topics and areas being developed by the students, suggesting different strategies for different types of data collection and interpretation. Some students may create a booklet, others a quiz, and still others a PowerPoint demonstration. Yet all of them need to revise, be aware of the audience's needs, and work with peer and teacher feedback. Teachers can discover all kinds of topics for mini-lessons and demonstrations from students who are writing in different genres and on various topics, yet the class can learn together about the craft of writing.

What does "creative writing" mean? Isn't most writing creative?

For decades, most creative writing was fiction or poetry, but as we came to understand how texts function, we realized that most writers are creative in their word choices, their styles, and their structures. A biography of Martin Luther King or a history of the Second World War may not be creative with events and facts, but the style and structure are wide open to different approaches. Today, we tend to look at the genre or the author's intent for the writing. If we focus on narrative fiction, much of the fiction students consume is about action-driven plots. Teachers, by offering students other models in their reading, and by leading mini-lessons that focus on different attributes of effective fiction writing, may be able to move their fiction writing into new areas. I am always attempting to find ways of helping young writers create fiction that is more than a series of exciting plot twists. Donald Graves says that the secret may lie in giving the students strategies for developing characters who in the writing are beginning "to understand other people, themselves, and the human condition."

We can hitchhike along with the writers and artists who have motivated us into action, taking off from their initial creations but making the work our own. We can transform a selection of print into another mode, take the essence of the text and rework it into another form, such as rethinking an excerpt from a novel as a poem. This often necessitates shifting the point of view, and may lead to a deeper understanding of the text that is being patterned. Retelling is another way of transforming print. Both oral and written retellings permit students to reveal their ideas about what the text means to them, encouraging imaginative and personalized recreations of the original. Patterns and shapes for writing can present creative frames that help us to order or arrange our ideas.

Are shared writing and interactive writing the same thing?

In a sense, they are the same: students compose a text together with the teacher. Shared writing may involve students writing a collaborative letter of thanks to a class visitor or generating a chart of group findings. The teacher acts as scribe and talks about the writing process as the students contribute their ideas to the composition of the text. The teacher discusses alternatives and takes suggestions from the students on what to write. Shared writing is writing *with* students.

Interactive writing is a cooperative event in which teacher and students jointly compose and write text. Not only do teacher and students share decisions about what they are going to write, they also share the duties of the scribe. The teacher guides this process and provides appropriate pacing, assistance, and instruction when needed.

Both processes involve the cooperative constructing of a common text.

I enjoy shared and interactive writing as demonstrations for older students as well. The class generates ideas that the theme or topic suggests; then I write in point form on the blackboard phrases chosen by the class. In the example below,

Donald Graves was such an influential educator in supporting changes in the teaching of writing in schools. I found it helpful to reread his book *Writing: Teachers and Children at Work, 20th Anniversary Edition*, in rethinking my own ideas for written communication.

these points serve as the basis for developing poetic images and thoughts by the students. For my eighth-grade classroom my supervisor Bill Moore demonstrated this method with a topic suggested by the students, and a piece of poetry writing was created as a model for composition.

Subject: poplar trees at night in autumn
Images suggested by students:
1. Spider webs across the moon.
2. The boughs of the leafless trees interlace like the threads of a web.
3. They set traps to catch the moon.
4. I want to break the web and let the moon escape.

Images morphed into a poem by students:

TREES AT NIGHT

> The trees weave magic webs across the moon
> With interlacing boughs,
> Like giant spiders setting traps
> To catch a tasty morsel.
> Moon, shall I break the threads
> And let you go?

How should I help in a writing conference?

The goal of any writing conference is to support the students' writing development. We need to act first as wise and compassionate readers, then instructors and editors. I have worked with hundreds of graduate students, mainly teachers, and they have represented as complete a range of abilities as any grade in any school. Most need help in choosing and focusing on a topic; most need help in finding resources to support their projects; most need help in revising their ideas, rearranging sections, moving chapters, adding and clarifying details, finding references to support their opinions and validating final drafts.

Eddie Ing devotes a great deal of time conferring with small groups of children in his primary class who are working on a collaborative retelling of a folktale. He uses his prompts to help them return to the story, to decide on how many illustrations will be required, to determine what text will accompany the drawings. They will meet again as the work progresses, and time becomes his ally as students rethink their attempts two days later. Then, after two weeks, their work is completed, and he binds and laminates the books for the classroom library. The results are the students' work, and he was merely the helpful advisor, prompting them toward success.

PROMPTS TO USE IN WRITING CONFERENCES

What are you working on? Do you want help with your writing? I'm interested in this idea. Tell me more. Why did you want to write about this topic? Have you changed your mind while working on this topic? What do you see in your mind's eye? What do you want the reader to remember about your piece? What is the most important point you are trying to make? Do you think you have more than one topic here? What is your favorite part? Could you cut a piece out and use it in

Lucy Calkins has helped many teachers grow stronger as reading and writing educators with her institutes and her books. *One to One: The Art of Conferring with Young Writers*, written with Amanda Hartman and Zoe Ryder White, will give teachers a careful and supportive means of working in conferences with their students.

another project? What about looking back at your idea web or your brainstorming chart, or refining a new direction? Do you need to find more information? Where did this event happen? What caused this event? Would a reader understand this part? Can you expand this description? Can you add your own reactions and feelings? Why does this part matter? Do you think a reader will care about this character? Will a reader hear your own voice? Read your lead aloud. Will it work for a reader? How to you want the reader to feel at the end of the piece? I am having trouble understanding this part. Can you help me to clarify it? Have you thought of trying another pattern? What about chunking the lines in your poem differently? Do you think any illustrations might help? Read this quotation aloud to me. Does it sound like real people talking? Would adding some dialogue help in this section?

Can I help students in editing and revising their writing?

Yes, but it is not always a simple process. When I learned that revising and editing were two different processes, I changed my way of working with student compositions. We need to make students aware that what most interests us about their writing is what they have to say, not just their typos and errors. Editing is about correcting errors in grammar and spelling, and we teachers may spend too much time focusing on it; revision deals with larger issues such as flow of narrative or ideas, relevance of information, logic, and clarity of expression. These are more difficult to categorize as "correct" or "incorrect," but they are vital. And we can be constructive and positive in suggesting changes here rather than being critical.

Students may be motivated to refine and polish their work when they are preparing it for an authentic audience. To assist them, we can have a variety of writing resources, online and in print, available in the classroom: dictionaries, thesauruses, computer centres, word games, and quotations by famous authors and poets. Writers often benefit from leaving their writing for a day or two. A fresh reading often highlights necessary changes. All students need to see themselves as writers. Sharing a published piece by each student in the classroom at various points in the year is a positive reinforcement for their work.

- As a demonstration, you can select a piece of draft writing that needs revising from a student's portfolio from a previous year, or create a piece of writing that demonstrates the specific editing issues you want the students to examine. Transcribe it onto a screen or make individual copies. Then, in small groups, the students can read the piece as editors and indicate where revision is needed. To model the editing process, incorporate their suggestions by crossing out, adding, and deleting information.
- It often helps if you monitor your students' work, and look for an example that documents the various stages of the revision/editing process. With the author's permission, you can display his or her drafts to illustrate the revision process to others. Students can then examine the drafts and use them as models for their own writing.
- If you share your own draft writing with the students, they can offer suggestions for improvement. Having the chance to see you — the teacher — revising your writing helps them understand the reasons we all have for revision.

During a visit to our faculty by the British poet Gareth Owen, he was asked a question about improving students' writing. One simple suggestion he offered was to place prompts around the room that could act as support cues for young writers. He mentioned that, after he demonstrated a list of clausal conjunctions to his class, their writing structures altered almost immediately. Lately, Ralph Fletcher has helped us all look more carefully at the elements of writing, and we now know a variety of strategies that we can open up to our students:

- finding the appropriate voice;
- selecting a genre that supports the purpose for writing;
- reviewing favourite books to note the authors' techniques;
- making good word choices — precise nouns, strong verbs, effective adjectives and adverbs — not always the first word that flows from your pen;
- including all necessary information;
- replacing overused words like "nice," "said," "a lot," and words you have repeated often;
- looking up synonyms for a word in a thesaurus, and using an unusual word you have discovered;
- finding a rhyming word in a rhyming dictionary;
- using an effective metaphor or simile;
- using a variety of sentence types that flow well, combining them where possible, and eliminating sentence fragments;
- clarifying ideas that are vague;
- adding important details;
- showing rather than telling, by describing actions and events;
- sequencing ideas and eliminating repetition or unnecessary ideas or information;
- describing the setting;
- incorporating natural-sounding dialogue;
- giving necessary background;
- developing a character fully;
- creating careful transitions in time and place to help the flow of the writing;
- using flashbacks and flash forwards when appropriate;
- choosing a powerful lead;
- having a strong conclusion;
- choosing an effective title.

Are writers' notebooks still useful?

I am still impressed when I visit a class where students keep notebooks or journals filled with their thoughts and ideas, reflections and dreams, observations and quotations. For many, electronic devices have replaced notebooks, but I was given a beautifully designed one this year by my editor, with my name embossed on it. It requires no battery. My granddaughter has started writing in a small leather-covered notebook that I gave her. At seven, she values her notebook. We can encourage students to reflect on their writing in their notebooks, but what they write should be up to them. These suggestions might help them get started:

- Write about special events at home.
- Notice the unusual behaviours of your pets.
- Sketch your observations of happenings at school and at home.
- Glue in a special poem or letter.

- Remember moments from a holiday or camp.
- List books and films you have enjoyed.
- Remember characters and incidents in books you have read.
- Write down memorable quotations.
- Include photos of friends and family.
- Retell family stories.

- Freeze a moment in time.
- Jot down an idea for a story.
- Create a web of ideas about an interesting issue.
- Remember conversations with others.
- Get something off your mind or work through a problem.
- Record your hopes and dreams.

What kind of feedback should I give about a student's writing?

> Feedback acknowledges where they are in the learning process. They know what the goals are, and also know that they can obtain meaningful feedback as a scaffold towards increased success. This can be in stark contrast to an assessment that might only show what a student does not know, or what they failed to pick up in the lesson. The Feedback-Friendly classroom harnesses the 'talk' and conversations that happen to help build stronger academic, developmental and social foundations for success.
>
> Deborah McCallum, *The Feedback-Friendly Classroom*

The ability to advise a writer about their work develops over time. Working with teachers who are graduate students presents similar difficulties, but when the discussion helps, both parties are grateful. My colleague Shelley Stagg Peterson has explored issues of feedback in her research, the teacher's as well as peers', and has found these suggestions to be helpful:
- Feedback should be given in the spirit of showing student writers the positive effects their writing is having on readers like us.
- Identify areas where students could revise their writing to clarify meaning or more fully engage readers.
- Students should always feel that they can use the feedback in their own way, that the feedback is suggestive, rather than prescriptive.

And peer feedback can be helpful, but students do need guidance in learning how to support fellow writers:
- When the writer feels blocked, peers and the writer can play with ideas to move the writing forward.
- Peers can ask for clarification about what they find confusing or identify missing information.
- Peers can give their emotional response to the writing (for example, pointing out where it makes them laugh).
- Peers can question how plausible particular events or ideas are.

Peers may not, however, be the best providers of criterion-based feedback regarding conventions because they often lack the needed grasp of conventions. Their feedback should be valued for the information it provides about how readers respond to a piece of writing. Teacher feedback is generally more useful for moving students along in their use of writing conventions.

Does spelling count?

Doreen Scott-Dunne, in *When Spelling Matters*, offers specific techniques for teaching students ways and means for understanding how words work, and how spelling can be a problem-solving process.

Yes. A "good" speller knows when a word is a problem, and how to go about solving the spelling: remembering other similar words, making online or print spelling checks, or even asking a partner. We want to encourage students to use all the different strategies available for examining how printed texts work, to explore the practical details of language, responding to the pieces of language as artifacts, as text etymologists. I need spell checks, online dictionaries, and other references in my own work; most people do.

Word walls with different categories, sorting and categorizing words, word searches, word puzzles, reading silly poems full of word play, cloze exercises, supplying magnetic letters and word board games, all help students to notice how words work. Becoming an effective speller is a gradual process, and we may need to explicitly direct the student to focus on a few words at a time, words connected by structure or pattern, so that word knowledge can be incremental. In our classrooms, some advanced students will be working with dozens of unrelated words, but students in difficulty will need our help in taking just a few words apart and putting them back together. We need to focus on one word that leads to three or four more. Classifying their errors from a piece of writing may help them to understand a particular spelling pattern.

Don't be afraid to focus on word power at times in their reading, their writing, and their projects. I believe that *Word Power* should be a special period each week where students explore the mechanics of language, special words or phrases, dialect, jargon, etymology of words, phrases, metaphors, patterns, symbols, word play or games, puzzles, sentence structures, archaic or new words and expressions. In doing so they are exploring the "bones" of text, investigating how language is constructed. We must remember that word power is cumulative and lifelong, and aim for significant individual growth from year to year.

- Writing is the best way to learn about spelling.
- Computers or multiple copies of different dictionaries are useful for students looking up word information.
- Games such as Scrabble and cooperative word-building activities (e.g., how many words a team can make from the letters in *onomatopoeia)* can help students see how words work.
- Students can be responsible for locating interesting word games online and preparing them for classmates. They can find activities that explore derivations, prefixes, homonyms, mispronounced words, silent letters, compounds, when or when not to double letters, contractions, irregular verbs, and mistakes on ads or signs.
- I found a list of four hundred homophones online today; too many to remember, but a great resource for creating a game called "Which word?"

When I go to a restaurant with my grandkids, we take resources along and hope for a free placemat with word games. Lately, Mara and I have been playing a word game, not unlike those on television. She writes down a word but with missing letters, and I have to guess the word. Recently she offered –n-p-r-t-o-a-, and I tried valiantly to decipher it, but to no end. She announced, "It's *inspirational*." How much fun spelling words can become!

Should I still teach grammar?

Research today tells us that students learn about language by using it and then by noticing how it is used. Learning when to use standard and nonstandard English depends on the context of the situation. We usually speak the way our community speaks, and to alter language patterns requires creating a positive community environment and encouraging frequent interaction with significant models — speakers, coaches, peers — and, of course, listening to and reading stories and poems, incorporating patterns in our storytelling and writing.

However, it is useful for students to examine language, detecting differences in their own oral and written language forms, as well as observing the language used by authors. Students can benefit from knowing common terms, such as *noun* and *verb*, when discussing how language works so that they can add knowledge about English to their language repertoire. Just finding slang or unusual expressions in a novel can turn students on to language awareness.

The problem for us is that we need to find alternate ways of introducing information about usage and grammar to students, rather than repetitive drill exercises or parsing of simplistic sentences so that the information can be understood and used in their own work. Many teachers have found engaging games and activities online that promote an awareness of how language works, and students are more effective writers when word and sentence knowledge supports their text constructions.

- There are websites that explore run-on sentences, sentence fragments, compound sentences, pronouns without references, etc.
- Word power is cumulative and always growing. I enjoy collecting headlines from different newspapers, especially sports headlines. The text has to be minimal and terse, words are used for maximum effect, and they are often in a different syntactic structure than usual, with coined phrases, nouns as verbs, and so on. Some students will be able to explain each headline; others will need support. Such are the ingredients of comprehension: knowledge of content, style, syntax, vocabulary, and readers' interests.
- Sentence expansions and variations open students' awareness of patterns:
    Birds sing; birds sing in the spring; did you know that birds sing in the spring?
    Students can build simple, compound, and complex sentences.
    They can try beginning a sentence with a noun, a verb, an adverb, a phrase, etc.

How do I incorporate literacy strategies into inquiry projects?

This method of student engagement is actually changing how classrooms function. Student-driven inquiries and investigations can grow from a class topic or an issue drawn from the students' own interests that stimulate their curiosity and cause them to want to find answers or solutions. Research can grow from science or social studies as well, or from the themes in novels and picture books. These inquiries can last for a few days or several weeks. Students can identify a topic, formulate questions, and develop a plan of research. Intensive long-term research projects immerse the students in authentic reading and writing experiences, and

Gail Tompkins' book *50 Literacy Strategies* presents succinctly and insightfully strategies for literacy growth in all subjects.

Inquiring Minds Learn to Read and Write by Jeff Wilhelm and colleagues offers practical suggestions for implementing an inquiry approach with students.

we can help maintain their interests and sustain their efforts as we help in planning and offer ways to sort, select, and arrange data.

Events in which students present their inquiries offer opportunities for both oral communication and written and visual demonstrations of the research. I am impressed by the power of technologies to cause students to carefully consider how they will present their findings. Websites and bulletin boards let other students benefit from research, and young investigators may want to distribute a guide sheet for observers to note their learning and to ask further questions. The inquiry approach encourages engagement if student voices are significant factors in determining topics and issues to be explored.

Evaluation rubrics are useful for letting the students reflect on their learning processes, and for recording the types of writing and research they explore. This is a good opportunity for setting standards that actually affect how others will view the work: using media effectively; presenting information neatly with careful handwriting or computer printing; arranging graphic displays artistically; using captions and headings to stimulate interest and to give cohesion to the study.

In the course of completing an in-depth study of a topic of interest, students will have explored the types of reading and writing that will be valuable throughout their school years and in their future lives, engaging in authentic inquiries in order to discover and communicate their findings. It may be the first time students recognize that the processes of reading and writing occur in the content subjects, and that they need to see themselves as readers and writers when they are involved in subject disciplines. Literacy does not only raise its head in language arts; it is a lifelong interpreting and constructing process.

Should I stay away from controversial issues in my choices of inquiries?

Honest inquiries will often focus on complex issues, and that may be one of the reasons for their success with students: they have choice in some aspects of the topics, they can work independently, with a partner or a group, and the process takes time and commitment. I would hope that these young researchers would seek out information, explore issues of social justice, broaden their outlooks, and not settle for simplistic opinions. Working with two teachers of seventh- and eighth-grade students a while ago, I was so impressed with the strength of their students' research abilities and findings, their passion for what matters in our world. Their words could act as mentor texts for all of us engaged in discovering real reasons for exploring issues deeply and personally:

> In Geography, what better way to learn about factors that influence migration than to study the way of life of people that immigrate to our country? We have made Uganda our case study. We studied the peoples' way of life, the 25-year conflict, their cultures, and their customs much like any other class, but we supplemented that learning by connecting with students in the heart of the conflict, We wrote letters and communicated with former child soldiers, and we interviewed people who fled their home country to start a new life in ours.
>
> Our class was moved and motivated by these experiences and wanted to do more. We took this opportunity to learn about economics and sustainable solutions. We compared our economy to theirs and used it to answer questions such as, why doesn't everyone go to school in Northern Uganda

and how has Canada been involved in the problems and solutions in a country so far away? We discovered that buying goods here and shipping them to Uganda, even with the best intentions, could have dire consequences by affecting local businesses and economies. We found sustainable solutions to problems, while also supporting businesses and families in Uganda.

Kevin Sebastion

Kevin and Jeff describe in detail their excellent classroom programs promoting social justice in my book *Caught in the Middle.*

We need to focus on big ideas and challenging questions. World issues, environmental and scientific challenges, social justice, and character-based big ideas are great topics to start with, and the new Science and Social Studies curriculum guides are filled with excellent examples. Over this past year, our division had three phases within our program and many big ideas to investigate:

- *What Does the World Look Like to Me?*
- *Where Do I Fit into the World?*
- *How Can I Use My Voice to Influence the World?*

Within these areas we investigated many interesting and thought-provoking issues, including human reliance on fossil fuels, consumption, consumerism, and how the economy works, what it means to be a hero, what makes us who we are and how we want to live, and even the notion of competition versus cooperation.

Jeff Demacio

What about video and computer games played in school?

Many parents are still nervous about their children playing computer games in school. As in everything, balance matters, but computers, in one form or another, are part of the daily lives of most students. There are dozens of games that can be played onscreen using the Internet or prepared programs. With the computer, children can search and discover several games, then make a "game plan" for others to follow, keeping track of the results or printing the outcomes.

Board games such as Pictionary and Scrabble, which involve reading and spelling, can motivate students and encourage learning, and can also be used in cooperative learning lessons to encourage working in groups. A principal I know purchased twenty board games last summer for his middle school classrooms. As I mentioned earlier, my son plays a board game with his two children (ages five and seven) almost every evening after dinner. They must have fifty of them. I have watched the two children read and count in ways with games that I could not imagine with school texts.

Playful approaches and games may be among our strongest allies. Computer programs are beginning to offer us intriguing ways to build word strength with spelling and vocabulary games and puzzles, as well as offering support for struggling handwriters and spellers. It is significant that many of the games onscreen offer openings to limited readers for taking part in print-based activities, with less frustration and defeat than in much paper-and-pencil work.

In *Literacy and Education*, the new literacies authority James Gee says that many features of electronic games facilitate learning:

- they allow players to take on a new identity;

- they are interactive, and players must perform some action in order to receive feedback;
- they are scaffolded into well-ordered problems;
- players form hypotheses and gain competencies in the early stages of a game that will be used and built on in later stages;
- they promote learning: they offer multiple ways to learn, provide an opportunity for active learning, and encourage experimentation and discovery.

How do I find interesting topics for writing explanations and procedures?

Explanatory types of text include research reports, experiments, essays, and inquiries. The trick is to make the topics engaging and useful. A few years ago, while working on a genre study involved with reading and writing instructions, I asked eighth-grade students to remember a time when they wished they had had an instructional manual of some type to help them with a task that had caused them some difficulty. Philip, who had been working with me on Saturday renovating a house, decided to incorporate that experience into his writing. He reminded me that the strongest topics for writing are life-centred, where our words are energized by our experiences.

HOW TO REMOVE PLASTER FROM A WALL

I'm going to discuss three major parts of this time-consuming job: preparing, removing, and other problems of removing plaster from a brick wall.

The first and most important thing you should do is cover everything with plastic. The dust is terrible.

Next, make sure you've got a pair of safety goggles and a safety mask. The goggles are used to protect your eyes from small bits of plaster. It's painful and takes forever to get particles of plaster out. It is also harmful to your eyes. The mask is used to keep the dust out of your lungs. The best masks are the type with changeable filters. The only thing you might want to wear is a hat to keep plaster out of your hair.

What do you use to remove the plaster? Your hands? Maybe. However, the best tool to use is a regular hammer. Do not use a sledge hammer. They are too heavy to swing. The weight slows it down and you'll just mark the wall. And even if you are able to get a good swing you will most likely put a hole in your wall. Wooden-handled hammers are better than rubber-handled hammers; they won't cause your hands to blister.

Now you're ready to start. You swing the hammer, hit the wall and nothing happens. Why? The easiest way to remove the plaster is by angling the hammer when you make contact with the wall. It doesn't matter where you start. Once you get going it becomes very easy. Hint: it's best to hit the wall about five inches from the previous blow; the plaster should come off faster. The only problem with this task is if you plan to play baseball the next day; you'll find out it's quite painful to pick up anything, such as a bat. There is no way to avoid this problem. Your hands will be the same as usual after a couple of days.

So the best of luck in your task. One other thing I should mention: if you ever work for a man named Booth, and he wants you to do some plaster removal, he'll probably tell you it's a two-hour job. Don't believe a word of it. The job will most likely take you at least six hours.

How do I help students write "informed" opinions?

Starting with a story in the "George and Martha" series by James Marshall, the students in one grade-two class decided to write advice to George. Most of the selections begin in the first person, although there was no instruction to do so from the teacher.

> I advise you to make your own food so you won't say to each other I don't like this and go to restronts alot and if one of you are ill ask him or her what you would like and how they wont it made thats what I say.

> I understand your problem you ought to tell Martha about the soup or just say I don't want that today. If you feel that way about Martha. Why don't you marry then it would be easer to tell her don't you think. I am sure you will get along with each other. I would try some more flavors of soup it could be tasty.

> You should not be angry you should tell them to be friends maybe marry live together. Or spend a holiday together. Buy presents for each other by happy enjoy life. Meet people. They should never disagree.

> I advised George to tell Martha every time if there was any trouble. I advised Martha never to give George Split Pea Soup again.

> All you have to do is to tell Martha the truth because she will find out later. You should live together because will make a nice couple. Martha would make you cook.

We shared these helpful opinions, and the students decided they needed to know more about the two characters before selecting one group response, so we found five books in the series, and the students read them in five groups and subsequently made a large diagram of the two characters and listed what they had found out about each. They finally decided that the two would not marry but would just be friends, so they should share their feelings.

We want readers to carefully weigh evidence in order to make thoughtful decisions regarding their own opinions, to combine textual information with their own background knowledge. This moves the discussion into the area of argument, when students need to draw conclusions and apply logical thought to substantiate their interpretations. Most of all, we want readers to make and to recognize informed opinions. Young readers need to be trained to recognize persuasive writing and use judgment as they read it. This type of text includes letters to the editor, reviews, debates, arguments, advertisements, and persuasive articles. How real can we make them? If you need ideas to begin with, the *New York Times* online lists five hundred topics it offers for its student contests. It may help to remember that persuasion is concerned less with supportive data than with an argument, which is more evidence-based.

What topics can be the focus for writing nonfiction articles?

Writing reports, articles, and editorials offers young people opportunities for incorporating both information and their own personal perspectives and viewpoints into their writing projects. They can collect data and observations about issues and concerns that interest them in their school lives and in their community, and then add their own comments using their own voice. Informed opinion is the heart of an effective column, and students in the middle years are certainly ready at the drop of a hat to share their opinions on almost any topic. Sharing this type of writing often results in useful feedback, and the original ideas continue to develop and grow.

We can use these types of activities as sources for writing projects, working toward two basic goals: the need for informed opinion, and the struggle to become aware of the differences between fact and opinion. These are especially difficult areas as there are so many different viewpoints about contemporary issues. However, we can find many instances where opinion writing can be useful to developing writers: advertisements and commercials, reviews, letters, advice columns, speeches, editorials and debates. The Internet can be invaluable as a resource for examining complex issues, and of course for providing grounds for discussing the factual validity of the information.

The students in Nancy's seventh- and eighth-grade class participated in a community service project during the year. Their experiences served as significant resources for their independent writing projects. They were asked to write an article for a magazine, and this student, who was volunteering with the organization Meals on Wheels, used a narrative style for his report about his first visit with a client, Henry:

> "Kablaaaam!!!!" I stood up straight to ease my back. These trays were not light. After all the trays were organized, the checklists double confirmed, the groups assembled, the routes overlooked and everyone quiet, there were orders from the director to collect our trays and head out to our cars. Once we were settled in Sammy's 2000 silver Hyundai two-door sedan, we headed out to deliver lunches. Our first delivery was to a man named Henry. The short trip there was filled with a good laugh when Sammy and Frank started popping jokes at each other. They were funny guys; all was going well, but the laughter was about to stop...
>
> I didn't know what to expect walking up the eroded steps with a tray and a small carton of milk in my free hand. Frank came with me and as we approached the door Frank said, "Zis iz a very sad man."
>
> I looked at the front of the house before knocking on the door. There was a rotting piece of plywood that was peeling from the façade and there were a noticeable number of cracks and holes in his thick wooden door. There was no handle on the door just a nailed piece of two-by-four.
>
> Frank stepped forwards and knocked on the door. "Klunk, klunk!" There was a pause, then the door was opened. There stood a man, around 50 years old. He was wearing a pair of oversized dirty blue sweatpants, held up by a piece of yarn. He had on a stained white and blue striped dress shirt that was missing half of its buttons. His hair was greyish brown and it was long (shoulder-length) and matted. He looked like a skeleton because his face was very pale and bony.

"Hi, there!" he exclaimed.

"Hello. Come in please, come in," he said in a very weak voice.

As Frank and I entered, we were blanketed with darkness. We were standing in a short, skinny hallway that led to a staircase. To our left was a wall. To our right there was a dark room in which I could make out a foldout couch with a thin blanket on it. It was very cold and I doubted whether he had any heaters, or if he even had electricity.

I handed him the lunch tray and the milk and he thanked me with a kind voice.

"Goodbye," said Frank, as we stepped outside into the cool winter air.

"Goodbye," Henry replied, as he shut his paper-thin door and retreated to his cold, musty, foldout couch bed.

We returned to Sammy's 2000 silver Hyundai two door sedan and drove away.

How can I make poetry appealing to students?

Bob Barton and I have included many ideas for reading and writing poetry in our book *Poetry Goes to School*.

Each of us has had in school at some time the strangulating experience of analyzing a poem or a story to death, until by the end of the lesson we have lost whatever appreciation we had for the selection. Often the teacher, myself included, felt this to be a necessary building block for future independent learning, but seldom did many of the students internalize the learning so that they could use it later.

On the eve of my son's graduation from eighth grade, I found him awake in bed at one in the morning, reading the yearbook from his grades seven and eight. It was a collection of work from writing workshops that the teacher, Nancy Steele, had collated into a booklet, but what Jay was reading and rereading represented the lives of the classmates he had been with for those two years. Their writings were mainly poems; somehow Nancy had been able, in her carefully structured program, to offer this genre to her students as a means of capturing their very beings at this stage of adolescence. Their emotional swings, their shocking observations of the adult world, their new awareness of strong feelings — all seemed to fit inside the shapes of poetry that she modeled and shared with them.

Recently, while waiting for my car to be tuned at the auto dealership, I noticed the young man sitting beside me reading a poetry anthology, poems by Joseph Brodsky. I couldn't help but ask him about his choice of reading material, and he told me he was a professional bass player who had just moved to my city and found that poetry was a great calming influence during this transition in his life.

We need to incorporate poetry into the literacy lives of students, to open up reflective and emotional responses, and to demonstrate the power of language. Choose poems your students will want to hear, to read, to work with. Go online to search for them, take anthologies from the library, have the students begin the quest for poems that matter to them. Read blogs by teachers like you, and ask for suggestions. You will soon have a bank of poets and poems that will continue to live in your students' memories.

I live in fear
that I
will teach the poem
and they
will lose the poet
and the song
and the self
within the poem.
I live in fear
that I
who love the poem
and the children
will lose the poem
and the children
when I teach the poem.
But I will teach the poem
Live with the fear
Love the children
And know the poet
is beside me
Just as afraid
But full of hope.

When students pattern a poem, are they really writing?

Years ago, after working with my friend Larry Swartz's class of sixth-grade students on poems about nature, I wrote them a small poem and mailed it to them as an expression of gratitude.

Somewhere in the woods
Stands a tree near the stream
Stares an owl in the night
Shines the moon on the rise
Sits a mouse near his hole
Soars the feather on the wing
Strikes the victim of the night
Sings the cycle of the world
Set inside the silent woods.

True to his professionalism as a teacher, Larry used that poem as a resource for more and more writing. I soon received a booklet of poems his students had written, patterned after a shape of their choosing, each poem beginning with "I am," and all connected to the theme of our impressions of nature. And yet the patterned formats of their poems somehow freed them to use words in different ways, to structure the lines in unusual ways, and to explore how they could mold their ideas into new shapes, which would in turn alter their messages. We have, in much of our teaching, underestimated the power of patterns for capturing thought.

THE OWL AND THE MOUSE   *TIGER*

I am the owl	I am the Tiger.
Sleeping in the day	I am stripes streaking
howling in the night	I am sun running
I am the owl.	I am the Tiger Cousin of Lion
I am the mouse	Brother of Panther
hunting in the day	Father of Lynx
dying in the night	I am the Tiger.
I am the mouse.	

                                            Sara

                  Jeffrey

Mentor texts, genres, formats and shapes offer us supportive structures for writing down our thoughts and feelings. We hitchhike along with the writers and artists who have motivated us into action, taking off from their initial creations but making the work our own. We can transform a selection of print into another mode, take the essence of the text and rework it into another form, such as rethinking an excerpt from a novel as a poem. This often necessitates shifting the point of view, and may lead to a deeper understanding of the text that is being patterned.

Should students read and write autobiographies? Life stories?

THE HUNGRY ALLIGATOR

Many, many years ago, when my grandfather was still alive, he used to work in the canals near the sugar cane fields in Guyana. He and his partner used to work very hard cleaning the weeds and grass out of the canals.
No people lived back in and around the hills and there was no access to transportation or anything else. So every morning, trucks would come around to take everyone to work and then, take them all back home in the evening.
   One day, my grandfather went to work with the other men as usual. He worked all day and when it was almost time to go home he had a small area in the canal to clean out. An alligator was hiding in the weeds and tried to grab him. The rest of the group helped him out, the angry alligator pranced around. My poor grandfather nearly died that day. He was bleeding a lot from all his wounds. When the truck arrived, he was taken to hospital. Grandfather couldn't walk for weeks and he was scared for a long time from his experience but he was thankful to be still alive.

                                    Sandy, grade four

It is the work of schools not only to pass on the stories of the past but also to encourage children to tell the stories of their own lives, the stories of their own making. For many students a respect for and understanding of story's central place in our lives may never have been fully valued. A student's identity, culture, and origins may be revealed in each story told, and the resulting experience will give the original tale a pattern and texture that will enrich both the teller and the told-to.

We can strengthen the students' story lives in so many ways:

- Make the classroom a safe place and a starting point for sharing life tales.
- Encourage spontaneous personal storytelling whenever it is appropriate.
- Ask students to connect their own experiences to what they have read about or listened to.
- Use special events — a touring play, a professional storyteller, a visiting guest — as opportunities for sharing memories stimulated by the experience.
- Use polished life tales as building blocks for sources for role play in a drama lesson.
- Help students use real-life stories as the basis for their fiction creations.
- Design opportunities for deep listening to the stories of others with a visit to a home for senior citizens or a hospice.
- Arrange for sharing stories with a buddy class of different-aged students in the school, or have a local high-school class come and tell polished life tales about their years in primary school.
- The teachers in my graduate courses talk and write about their literacy lives, and I am often moved by their recollections of their parents' interactions with books, the struggles of immigrant families who couldn't read in either their native or their new language, of homes where books were either invisible or sacred, where book learning was the only way to open doors. I hope that teachers will share some of their own life tales about literacy with their students. This kind of sharing makes us all part of the greater story of literacy.

How do responses using visual arts help with comprehension?

A few years ago I was involved in a literacy project in Florida, working with ninth-grade students and their teacher on changing the types of texts students with literacy difficulties were reading as part of their program. The school was replacing traditional reading texts with highly graphic magazine-format books filled with contemporary issues. I had visited the class three or four times and admired the reading teacher's open and compassionate way of being among her students. On my final visit, I interviewed the students in pairs, and each student wanted me to see their contribution to a large mural they had created celebrating the ten books they had read. The impact of the mural was powerful All the materials had been taken from media and magazines, and each component had been contributed by a proud student creator. Why did this composite art piece shine so brightly in their eyes? The size? The colours? The sense of pride it gave them as readers who had something to say without words? The arts are linked forever in literacy: we read pictures, cartoons, films, screens both big and small. We interpret and we construct, and we reinterpret and construct again.

In their book *For a Better World: Reading and Writing for Social Action*, Randy and Katherine Bomer say that learning experiences involving all the varieties of aesthetic knowing — visual arts, manual arts, music, drama, dance, poetry, personal stories — "are legitimate and potent ways of responding to social realities and acting on them."

Consider how your classroom program supports this: Are there times in the day when students are permitted and encouraged to express thoughts and feelings through the arts, to wonder aloud in conversation about a significant text, to hypothesize about a science project they are about to begin, to take risks solving a complex math problem that may require several attempts? Are they allowed to try and try again without feeling failure, but instead challenging their own puzzlements with imaginative efforts? We can notice and interpret the acts of imagination that enrich and extend everyone's learning. For readers of any age, images are part of the serious business of making meaning — partners with words for communicating our inner designs.

Students of all ages can draw along with their writing and their responses to stories. Linking visual with verbal modes of expression will result in better description and detail. There are many ways to see — teachers can capitalize on students' multiple intelligences. Creating visuals gives students a sense of freedom of expression because they feel less restricted by rules and convention than when they write without pictures, leading to poetic, complex, expressive, imaginative, reflective writing.

In a sketch-to-stretch exercise, students can draw their thoughts and responses as they read. The visuals can be used as a memory jog for discussions, or as journal responses. The drawings can be simple, such as stick-figures, and graphic-style text balloons can be incorporated.

Teaching for deep understanding means both understanding of the art forms and media within which we work and understanding of the complex world in which we live and create. In *Releasing the Imagination*, Maxine Greene helps us to better understand the role that imagination must play in our encounters of teaching and learning. Aesthetic education, for Greene as for many arts educators, speaks to our efforts to look at things as if they were otherwise, to imagine a more just, a more generous, a more artful world. In classrooms, we are engaged in this work daily.

In his middle-school classroom, David Mills selected important social issues and had his students connect emotionally to them through art, creating artistic pieces that illustrated their values and beliefs. "They created large banners in the style of Keith Haring, on a social justice theme of their choice. The finished banner is displayed together with the student-composed poem on the theme. Sharing the banners and poems on a gallery walk affirmed the importance of connecting literacy to visual arts."

Since I wanted to demonstrate the wide range of choices of response modes in this book, I asked Mairead Stewart if she would participate. At the time, she was a grade-eleven student at a school for the arts in Toronto. Mairead chose to create an art piece that captured the soul of the folktale. Here, she describes her creative process:

David Mills describes his interdisciplinary art program infusing social justice themes in my book *Caught in the Middle*.

For my response to "The Seal's Skin," I decided to draw how I felt about the story. My drawing is of the woman in seal form looking up at her daughter on one of her visits to see the children. I chose this particular image because my first response after reading the story was to wonder about the children and how they coped with everything. I wondered what they thought of their mother's sudden disappearance, and whether their father ever told them the whole story.

I guessed that the father hadn't told the children every detail because it was too painful for him to relive. Instead, the children figured out what happened on their own, and were able to sneak out to visit their mother when their father was away.

For me, this story was very sad. Everyone in the story ended up losing out in some way or another. The children lost their mother, the father lost his wife, and the woman lost her whole family. There were slight glimmers of a happy ending, though, and so I tried to show that in my drawing. Even though the mother lives in the sea, she is still able to visit her children and husband, and give them interesting things she finds. All in all, I really liked the story but wished it had a happier ending or a better message connected to it.

How can I use scripts as teaching texts?

Back in the days when I taught drama to seventh- and eighth-graders, we produced a play that two students, Ira and John, had co-written — *James Bond Meets Santa Claus*. They wrote fifty characters into their script, and we had an amazing time working on it and finally sharing it. To see how scripts were shaped, we found transcriptions from *Monty Python* and *Beyond the Fringe*, along with scenes from stage and film. The students read these aloud, and as they did their confidence and writing grew.

Even with all the attention popular culture gives the media, scriptwriting seldom appears in our writing programs. It may be thought of as too complex an activity, like writing a novel, but there are dozens of types of scripts we could consider. We need to decide if the work the students create is to be read aloud, or if the dialogue is simply a useful format around which we can structure our ideas, as in a poem in which the writer wants to isolate two voices.

In Nancy Steele's class, all students participated in a scriptwriting process. The students then selected twelve of the completed projects, cast them, and produced them for a parents' night. During that evening, plays were presented informally without labour-intensive sets and costumes, in three different rooms at the same time, as in a three-ring circus, and each visitor selected four of them to watch. I had the pleasure of attending several of Nancy's play nights, and I was always amazed at the level of writing and acting in these student-produced, informally presented scripts.

Scriptwriting is one of the best activities I have found for causing students to revise. It is not easy to write words that others can then give life to. If you can create a process where the writers observe their words being spoken aloud and then both hear and see the need for revision, the writing process is greatly enriched.

Transforming a text selection into script dialogue involves students in several literacy processes. For example, selecting part of a novel and turning the narrative into dialogue forces careful reading of the text and requires the writer to interpret the prose, maintaining the intent of the story and the characters while presenting the thoughts and actions through dialogue.

How do mind maps and other graphic organizers help promote literacy?

The structure of mind maps is similar to the way the brain sorts and stores information. These maps can help the brain organize ideas and think more creatively and can facilitate the development of metacognition, helping students to be conscious of their own thinking strategies during the act of problem-solving. Not only can mind maps deepen students' understanding of the concepts they are learning, but they can also provide opportunities for educators to gain valuable insight into their students' learning. Flow charts, semantic maps, graphic summaries, Venn diagrams, and lists can all be used both while students are reading and when they are finished and are preparing to share their new learning. These are transformative processes, re-presenting knowledge, and changing thoughts in the process of construction.

In addition to the traditional paper-and-pencil method of creating mind maps, there are now software programs that can be used to create mind maps electronically. Software programs like Inspiration and Smart Ideas allows students to create mind maps on screen. Students can choose from a large library of graphics to enhance their mind maps, as well as modify colour, shape, and font to add another layer of meaning to connections they make. This encourages learning in multiple modes and leads to a deeper understanding of concepts. Hyperlinks can be added to create multilevel maps, allowing students to link terms to other maps or insert more detail that can be accessed by clicking on the various nodes. Once a map is created, the program can convert the information to another format such as an essay outline. Venn diagrams can compare and contrast topics, characters plots, etc. Here is one example:

Plot Organizers

WAITING FOR THE WHALES
by Sheryl McFarlane

THE WHALE'S SONG
by Dyan Sheldon

Canadian Author
Grandfather
Little Girl's Mother
Time Passes
Little Girl Grows Up
Growth/Cycles
Birth/Death/Birth
Nature/Seasons
Loneliness
Love

Orca Whales
Grandparents
Granddaughters
Homes by the Sea
Beautiful Illustrations
Exact Settings and
Time Period
Unknown

British Author
Grandmother
Lillie's Uncle
Time Compressed
Songs
Myths
Stories
Dreams
Longing
Hopes

Some students who experience difficulty writing their book responses or summarizing their reading may benefit from presenting their material through the use of a graphic organizer. Educator Lucy Calkins reminds us to see this strategy as a way of making sense of the reading rather than an end in itself. It should be a rough draft of the reader's thinking and not a product to be mounted on the wall.

Semantic maps can be used during pre-reading to record students' thoughts about what may be in the text, emerging from a brainstorming or discussion session. This activity focuses on activating prior knowledge and connecting to personal experiences. One way to build a semantic map is to write a word that represents the main idea of the text in the centre of a piece of paper, then write related categories in squares that are attached to the main word. Students then brainstorm details related to the categories.

Should films, CDs, and visual arts be included as part of reading?

As I've already said, absolutely. All the strategies for literacy can be used in making meaning with a movie, or a painting by Vermeer, or a recording of poems about the Vietnamese War. We can examine these texts as we would print texts, sometimes in combination. We read reviews of a film, comparing the comments, and placing them alongside our own. We visit a large art gallery and seek out a docent to give us background to deepen the experience. Every senior class from sixth grade on should watch a documentary once a month, tied in with readings and YouTube programs and interviews. We can learn from all texts as we receive them critically and creatively; we become emotionally involved and cognitively aware, comparing, challenging, laughing, questioning, researching.

In a fourth-grade classroom, a boy stated that he had just read a novel on his own:

> DB: What was it called?
> Student: *Chasing Vermeer* by Blue Balliett.
> DB: What was it about?
> Student: These kids chased thieves who had stolen a painting.
> DB: Who was the painter?
> Student: I don't know.
> DB: Check the title.
> Student: Vermeer?
> DB: Right. What did the painting look like?
> Student: I don't know. There aren't any pictures in a novel (laughter).
> DB: No, but there are lots online. Hop down to the principal's office and use her computer and her colour printer, and see if you can copy six paintings by Vermeer.
> Student: Now?
> DB: Now.

Twenty minutes later, he came back to the classroom with six coloured prints of Vermeer's paintings, and a slew of information about the painter and Holland at that time, which he excitedly shared with the class. I asked him to tape the prints to the chalkboard, and then the students came up and examined them, trying to find the one that had been stolen. The novel reader said, "I know which one: 'The Lady Writing.'"

The student knew more about the book he had read, more about the context of the action, with new information about the background of the stolen image. The painting was indeed beautiful, and the fact that the woman in the painting was writing was not lost on the class's radar.

Years ago, I was running a film club for secondary students with Bob Barton and the National Film Board. Each Saturday we viewed a movie from the NFB archives, and then took part in an often spirited discussion of the film. One day we had watched a 1930 silent film, *All Quiet on the Western Front*. The film deals with German soldiers' extreme physical and mental stress during WWI, and it's a heart-wrenching story. At the end of the film, when the lights came on, I asked the group what they would like to talk about and a young man with a Hungarian accent said, "Sometimes nothing need be said." I agreed, and we left the room in silence.

We need to remember that texts include all types of communication, including pictures, photographs, films, and graphics. I like this list of prompts from the James A. Michener Art Museum in Doylestown, Pennsylvania, for students (or anyone) considering a painting as a text to be interpreted:

1. What do you see?
2. What did you see, hear or sense that made you say that?
3. Do you see more? What more can you find?
4. How does this work of art make you feel?
5. If you were the artist, how would you have made this? What different materials and processes would you use?
6. Does anything you see in this work of art remind you of something else you have seen or experienced?
7. What is this work of art about? Is there a message that goes beyond the subject matter?
8. What is the title of this artwork? How does the artwork relate to the title? If you could rename the artwork, what would your new title be?
9. Compare and contrast this work of art with:
   - another work of art in the Collection
   - another work of art you find while researching in a book or on the Internet
   - another work of art in a famous museum
   - an illustration you find in a book
   - a current events article
   - a story, poem, song or novel you have read, heard or written
   - an event in history
   - a famous person or someone you know
   - something you would find in nature
   - a modern or ancient invention
   - geometry, algebra or calculus
   - Anything! The possibilities for comparison are endless!
10. How does this work of art relate to you?

How is drama (role play, tableaux, ritual, playmaking) useful in literacy teaching?

A while back, I took part in a history lesson where the grade-seven class had been studying the building of the Canadian Pacific Railway across Canada. The teacher wanted to create some emotional connection to the minimal narrative in their textbook. I decided that the students should move into two groups, one as the board members deciding if they should continue giving funds to the project, and the other as the managers and foremen who were failing to handle an uprising by the Chinese workers, and who were at risk of losing their positions. We moved to the large meeting room in the school, and set up tables with the board at the head. Both groups were given time to prepare their questions and arguments, and then we began the improvised discussion. I acted as an unseen guide who could prompt and change scenes when required. The improvisation continued for forty minutes, and there were many passionate moments. Paul and Cody's responses summarize the work:

> Paul: We need to realize how many deaths are occurring. I'm not saying the Board's at fault. But we need to realize how many deaths are happening. We're supposed to be a free country where we let people from all over the world come to our country. If we don't care about other immigrants who come here to work and get killed, if we just say "Who cares? They're not from our country," people are not going to want to come here. People will think we're racist and that we don't care about any immigrants at all. We should have taken more time to make the railway safer.
> Cody: Now I feel guilty.

The students were deeply involved in their work, turning the text prose into effective oral statements.

My experiences inside classrooms have transformed me, moved me forward in some way, lifted or confused me, shocked or fulfilled me. For Maxine Greene reminds us in *Releasing the Imagination*, "We need to hold in mind the fact that arts experiences are almost inexhaustible. We can continue to return to each of the art forms that we create or perceive, diving into the deep end of the pool again and again. If these experiences have any richness, any density at all, there is always more." And in that "more" lies hope for a better world.

What are some drama strategies I could use in the classroom?

There are many ways in which we can involve students in developing and demonstrating their understanding of text through role-playing:

- What if we consider the texts we use as resources for role-playing? Which incidents from a text will students want to replay as partners, in groups, or as a class? How will they begin and end? Whom will they role-play? Shall we share a moment or two from their improvisations to see the unique retellings? Will we record the work with cameras or phones?
- Parallel texts. Having read a story, which incident in the plot will students use as the basis for their improvisation? They can move from the original text to a parallel story that grows out of their improvisation work. Doing so creates opportunities for comparing the two texts: the original and the new version.
- Moments in time. How will students capture dramatic moments in the text? Will they create a tableau, or frozen picture? Who will be in the tableau? Will there be a spoken caption? A sequence of tableaux?
- Physical representations. How will we help our students to express and represent their interpretations through a physical mode — that is, using their bodies in movement and dance to picture what their imaginations have

created? What music might they select to support their work, or could they incorporate drumming or singing as part of the movement?

- Research for role-playing. Finding information to strengthen and support role play through Internet searches for documents, books, and images will be a powerful asset in expanding and deepening the work. Who will be the researchers? Who will ask the questions?
- Sharing within a community. We want our students to experience presenting their work and sharing their creations. How can we help them prepare for their presentations to reduce tension and promote success? Will they use talking-point notes? Will they use PowerPoint visuals? Will they present to a small group?
- Writing in role. What opportunities can we provide for our students to engage in authentic writing? How can the letters, diaries, and documents they compose on a theme being explored serve as artifacts within the work itself?
- In character with technology. As technology becomes more available in our schools, we can participate in a blog or by email as characters-in-role discussing issues with one another. What scenes will we film so we can see the varied interpretations groups have developed? In what other ways can we involve technology in our active learning sessions?
- Interviewing. What part could role play have in helping students hone interview questions and develop spontaneous responses? Could students interview a character from the original text the group is reading? What if students develop their own interviewing situations from documents, history, or novels? Can we use technology to promote deeper involvement as we transcribe the interviews, or incorporate still photos of the speakers as their words are heard?

How do I begin using drama and role play with my class?

Working with Gini Dickie and her grade-six students in an inner-city school in Toronto, I was struck by the quality of the community she had created with her students and the level of literacy work they were achieving together. As part of an anti-bullying unit, I managed to provide each child with a copy of the novel *Silverwing* by Kenneth Oppel, which Gini began reading aloud to the class. It is a fast-paced adventure fantasy, full of cliff-hanging action, a perfect book to share with these students. Set in a fantasy world of a bat colony, it chronicles the perilous adventures of Shade, the runt of the Silverwing colony, who becomes separated from the others and must take a remarkable journey in order to rejoin them.

First visit:

I visited the class halfway through the reading of the book, and together we explored the adventures they were listening to. We chose scenes from the novel, and students improvised dialogue that might have occurred among the characters. We worked as a whole class, often in a circle, and different youngsters would participate during each scene. Because the book races along like an adventure film, there was great opportunity for developing the interactions between the characters.

Students volunteered to role-play the female bats who had to discipline Shade for endangering their entire colony with his antics. The dialogue took place inside the circle, with the student playing Shade standing in the middle. As they questioned him and tried to arrive at a just punishment, I was actually shocked at how much information they had absorbed from the teacher's reading of the text. In this scene and the ones that followed, the author's research — the bat lore and natural history — filled their talk and strengthened the tension and drama of the moment. No one had told them to memorize the details from the novel; they were using them spontaneously to move the action along, to deepen their roles, filling the room with the wingbeats of twenty-five Silverwing bats.

Second visit:

There were five secondary students in the classroom one morning as part of their cooperative learning project. When I teach, I need everyone participating, and so, with some persuading, the older students became the owls, enemies of the bats. They had to be persuaded to leave the bats alone, to let them migrate to Hibernaculum, their new home. In one powerful moment, the bats confronted the five owls, determined to know if they could trust them, and one grade-six youngster asked if he could examine an owl pellet to see if the remains were bat or rat. The high-school boy as owl mimed the regurgitation of the object with such skill that the class gasped as the grade-six student took it in his hand. Of course the pellet was imaginary, but he held it in his hand, looked at it, turned and pronounced, "Rat, not bat." The work continued.

Third visit:

When I later returned to the class, the reading of the book had been completed, and the students had chosen for me the name of Icarus. They lined up to present me with the stories they had previously told aloud, now written on dark purple paper with silver pens. As one by one they read to me their memory from the colony, I shook their hands and gave each a copy of the sequel novel, *Sunwing*. One girl asked: "Do you mean we can keep this book at home? This is my first book that is mine."

A postcript:

I found a Kenneth Oppel site on the Internet, along with dozens of questions for teachers to have their students answer after reading each chapter. But there was also a fine interview with the author that students would enjoy. Use manuals, even electronic ones, if you feel you need them, but be selective and professional in your choices. By the way — the secondary students each asked if they could have a copy of the novel.

Helpful prompts for structuring a story drama event

During the lessons I create with students, I hear myself using many of these statements and questions to help organize the action of the drama. These act as prompts for finding ways of rethinking and redirecting the work in progress. I may ask one student in role to clarify his or her position or I may ask a group to replay what they have created so that we as a class can interpret their suggestions:

- *(Repeating their words)* Is that what you said?
- Is that what you meant?
- What are the implications of what you have said?
- What are the implications of what you have done?
- What do others think about this character's actions?
- Show me the consequence of what he/she has said or done.
- Remind me of how this work began.

- What happened in the past that affected this action?
- Flash back to the incident...
- Flash forward to a future...
- Freeze the action so that we can all see what is happening.
- Ask someone about an action or a statement you saw or witnessed.
- Talk aloud and all at once about your responses to what has happened.
- In groups, revisit and replay the scene where...
- With a partner, explore what happens when...
- Create a frozen picture of...
- Alone, create the scene where....
- In a circle, one by one, comment on the story so far.
- In groups, draw diagrams of...
- I will be working in a role alongside you as...

Does writing in role strengthen reading and writing?

I can't stress too much how profoundly role play and drama can support writing activities, from reflective notebooks and letters to interviews and proclamations. Drama also provides opportunities for collective writing, in which groups collaborate on a mutual enterprise — cooperating in collecting data, organizing information, revising and editing — to be used in the eventual drama work. If students are engaged in the expressive and reflective aspects of drama, living through "here and now" experiences that draw upon their own life meanings, then the writing that accompanies the drama and the writing that grows out of it may possess the same characteristics and qualities.

Writing in role enables students to enter a new sphere of attitudes and feelings. As they try for a more complex imaginative understanding of what has happened in their drama, their writing often becomes more intense, more authentic.

WRITING FICTIONAL DIARIES

A grade-eight class had read *Tales from Gold Mountain* by Paul Yee, and I asked them to enter the lives of the immigrant Chinese workers who had built the railway across Canada. One of the students captured her learning in a fictional diary describing seven days of toil. Here is an excerpt that shows how much she had immersed herself in the mind and heart of one character:

> Day 1 This is my first day in Canada after spending 14 days on the ship that brought me to my new life in Canada. We arrived in British Columbia, which is a province of Canada. I am just waiting for the ferry to come and take me to the part of the railway that I am going to be working at. I have waited many hours so far and there is still no sign of it coming. I am very hungry because the food that we received on the ship was not good at all. I hope that they will feed us better when we are working on the railroad. So far I think that I have made the right decision coming to Canada so that I can make some money to send back to my family in China.

> Day 2 They took me to this shack and it was filled with all of the other Chinese workers. It is morning now so we are all waiting out by the docks for the ferry to come. In the distance we see the big stern wheeler coming towards us. As soon as it got to the docks we all got on the ferry and it

took us to our destination. On our trip I have seen many animals and few people. This country is so different from the one that I come from. It seems that everyone here has money and a place to live but in China many people have nothing and no place to live. It took us all day to get to the part of the railroad that we will be building. It is night time now and the only thing that I can see are tents and a few workers. We were shown to our beds which are in the tents. I thought that we would have been living in buildings rather than tents. They gave us dinner but it was only rice and dried fish. It wasn't much better than what we got on the ship coming here. I am already missing my family.

6

How do I develop a literacy community?

What are some strategies for creating a cohesive group?

My son went to a public "alternative" school for grades seven and eight, where the mandate for the combined classes was to build a community. Sometimes the grades worked on projects together, and sometimes they operated independently. Over the two years, I watched the power of students belonging to a school community, and this was evidenced at my son's graduation from grade eight. Each of the graduates was honoured by a grade-seven student, and as each speaker recounted the honouree's time in the school, he or she presented the graduate, boy or girl, with a rose. All of the grade-eight students were teary-eyed, as were teachers and parents. This ceremony marked the transition to adolescence for these youngsters, to high school, away from childhood. The biographical speeches, drawn from interviews and observations, were such a far cry from stilted public speaking events relying on memorized data; this was an authentic occasion for sharing carefully crafted reflections concerning those who now would leave the circle of that school. A significant literacy event.

Teachers can try to create a cooperative classroom culture of curiosity, inquiry, and discovery that can result in greater student engagement. The students in your class will each reveal divergent interests, abilities, cultures, and family backgrounds, but you can try to build a classroom community that encourages a cooperative and respectful atmosphere for all members. Literacy offers an opportunity for achieving these goals, as we need a forum for sharing its many facets: planning the day's schedule, discussing current issues, reading aloud significant literature, presenting interactive mini-lessons on the many different aspects of reading, listening to talks by guests such as authors. We often read independently, but our power as literate humans is acquired from the connections we make to the responses and comments of other members of the larger community.

Donna Styles has found many benefits to holding class meetings, with students' greater accountability for what they do chief among the benefits. In classrooms

Donna Styles's *Class Meetings* gives us practical techniques for bringing students together as we build a classroom community.

with regular meetings, discipline is a minor issue. Any problems are discussed in that forum, and the students determine how misbehaviour will be dealt with. When peers are noting poor behaviour and discussing it in meetings, students feel highly accountable for how they act. Class meetings also provide students with an opportunity to serve on committees and to plan and orchestrate fun-filled activities. Donna reports that — without exception — students love class meetings; furthermore, the approach works well for the inclusion of students with special needs.

When Eddie Ing was training a group of junior-level students to prepare for a Lego Robotic competition, he spent the first two weeks on team-building activities involving cooperative games, and only then did he move to the designing and building of the team's robot. His team preparation work paid off with a winning performance, and the students felt their success was due to the cooperative games played beforehand.

Effective teachers have always supported students with individual needs, abilities, and interests, but there is much that is good about working with the whole class some of the time. I think a viable classroom program includes:

- class discussions of the issues that arise from reading and research, planning of the week's schedule, modeling of strategy use (e.g., how to question a text or explore differing perceptions);
- introduction and exploration of whole-class units built around themes and genres;
- mini-lessons and demonstrations by the teacher; seminars with the teacher and students sharing information and ideas; and book talks featuring new resources;
- whole-class read-aloud sessions that allow for participation, discussion, the raising of relevant issues, and demonstrations of strategies for understanding;
- inquiry-based opportunities for students to become agents of their own literacy growth, selecting topics, collaborating with others, searching for data, conversing with others, refining their work and sharing the results;
- excursions, talks by authors and other guest speakers, celebrations of completed tasks, and other shared events that heighten students' sense of being part of a larger whole.

Are there times when the whole class should read a novel together?

While some school districts frown on whole-class novel reading, I find it can be beneficial to the literacy community if used occasionally and as a demonstration of how the community can explore a single text. You need to select a book that most students can read, or offer support to some struggling readers, such as having them listen to a recorded version first. I always think of this type of activity as a community-building event, and take time to incorporate a variety of response modes into the work. And of course most of us remember a teacher holding the class in a spell as he or she read one chapter at a time, serializing the narrative and garnering the attention of everyone. There really should be no rules, other than, "Am I helping these students grow as readers and writers?"

Consultant Janet Allen in her book *Yellow Brick Roads* has revisited sharing texts with older students by reading a novel aloud as they follow along with their own copies. Her readers' growth proved her belief that choosing the right texts for shared reading is critical to increasing their positive attitudes towards reading. Many of them confirmed that when the teacher stopped reading "good stuff," their interest in reading decreased, and when the teacher made them read on their own, it "was just too hard, so I stopped trying." As always a balance must be struck between reading needs and interest levels.

What role does "talk" play in literacy growth?

Today's schools are full of the sound of students talking, and I enjoy this change from only "question and answer" discourse. More than ever students are encouraged to talk to each other one on one or in groups, and to enter discussions during class meetings as they argue, debate, question, comment, and share personal experiences.

Talk is a dynamic medium for learning in all areas and at all levels of schooling, a tool that will increase not only students' knowledge, but their ability to inquire, argue, reflect, and make sense of information. We want school to be a place where students are permitted and encouraged to talk their way into learning, where thoughtful exploration is valued, and where conversation is a valued mode of exploration.

- Students have better opportunities for buying into their own learning if they have a voice in determining, organizing, structuring, and responding to the events occurring in their classrooms.
- We can include student voices and choices in selecting topics or texts of relevance, substance, and interest.
- Students need the collaboration of others in conversation and discussions to provide feedback that will lead them to understand what they are thinking, what they are saying, and the appropriateness of the language they are using to say it.

Student talk can take the form of: chatting, announcing, narrating, describing, explaining, informing, recounting, brainstorming, imagining, sharing, commenting, comparing, classifying, questioning, hypothesizing, predicting, opining, complaining, analyzing, applying, creating analogies, inferring, directing, reporting, persuading, rephrasing, rethinking and revising, decision-making, problem-solving, role-playing, reflecting, interpreting, reading aloud.

Teacher talk can take the form of: asking authentic, open-ended questions, altering power roles, organizing events so that quieter children's voices can be heard, facilitating, modeling, demonstrating, instructing, scaffolding, helping unpack large ideas, prompting, pressing for depth, monitoring, paraphrasing, enriching, summarizing, linking relationships and previous ideas, asking for evidence and verification, offering feedback, clarifying, restating, elaborating, challenging.

We know as teachers the difference between social talk (recess), task talk (literature circles), and rehearsed talk (readers theatre), and of course these various modes blend depending upon the activity. We can organize our classroom events and cue our students so that they learn how to participate effectively and appropriately in the specific situations where talk matters. There will be times when the classroom is filled with the buzz of workers, when the children chat in pairs, when they share in small groups, when they confer with us, and when they join in the reading of a script, melting the frozen words. As well, they will recognize the power of silence as students read their poems aloud, as we demonstrate a strategy, as a speaker visits the school. The talk dynamic filters into every activity.

When is brainstorming useful?

In brainstorming, students confront a problem, search for a solution, or try to answer a complex question. The goal is to have the students come up with a bundle of ideas that are generated by the collective thinking of everyone contributing, engaging with each other, listening, and building on other ideas, freed from immediate judgment. You can invest the class's energy in a short period of time, perhaps fifteen or thirty minutes of intense, energetic engagement. You can capture the ideas of a brainstorming session by acting as a scribe using a chart, a Smart Board or the chalkboard, and write down the ideas generated by the students. Every idea is recorded, and none is rejected. After the time is up, students can arrange the responses and add missing ones or eliminate those no longer deemed useful. I have used this strategy for years and appreciate the vigour of the ideating that happens.

Once I was working with an auditorium of seventh- and eighth-graders, and decided to read aloud this short, short story of which there are many versions:

> The last man on Earth sat at his desk. Suddenly he heard a knock at the door.

The openness of this brief science-fiction story can lead to endless brainstorming about who or what might have caused the knock. It can be motivating to see how many possibilities students can come up with in only five minutes. Be sure to permit no repetitions of categories (only one robot, one creature). On this occasion the group generated this list:

> *the wind, a meteorite, an earthquake, a woman, a child, God saying that it is time to go, a BlackBerry timer going off, the devil ready for his soul, a raccoon, a tree branch, his heartbeat, the Internet, his imagination, a zombie, a robot, an alien, his dream, an angel, his own spirit returning, an object that fell off his desk.*

How can I promote public speaking?

Having had to act as a judge at public speaking contests over the years, I really prefer that public speaking occasions grow out of regular classroom work rather than be legislated as a formal semi-memorized speech about a topic assigned to the student and presented to classmates who may have little interest in the subject. Rather, think of all the opportunities for speaking to an audience where listeners are anxious to listen because the information is interesting or necessary: classroom or school debates about school policies, seminars on curriculum issues that students have thoroughly researched, demonstrations of science experiments, poetry readings, drama presentations, sharing results from research inquiries with PowerPoints and videos, introducing and thanking a speaker in the auditorium, interviews on Skype and podcasts or in person. What if we had a different understanding of what speaking in public meant, and organized our events so that students were constantly involved in preparing, presenting, and reflecting on their active, engaged "talk" events?

Caleigh Dunfield took her sixth-grade class in New Brunswick on a field trip to the Huntsman Fundy Discovery Aquarium in St. Andrews.

> Through the guidance of marine biologists and interpreters, students learned about and experienced marine life directly. They held lobsters, touched

skates, examined real whale baleen, and, perhaps most notably, met two harbour seals. Naturally, our close proximity to the Bay of Fundy meant that a number of students had a personal connection to the fishing industry already. Many students were keen to share family anecdotes about poor weather, biggest catches, a misplaced sculpin hiding inside a rubber boot, painfully surprising an unsuspecting fisherman — you name it!

This prompted the idea of using our website to reach out to a working fisherman to discuss the line of work. We contacted fisherman and musician Mike Trask of Musquodoboit Harbour, Nova Scotia, who graciously agreed to respond to our questions between shifts on his lobster boat. Excerpts from our exchange with Mike appear below:

Do you fish with a rod or net?
When I fish lobster, I fish with a wooden lobster trap! We haul up 250 wooden lobster traps from the bottom of the ocean every day. If there's a lobster we take it out, then put fresh bait on the trap and then send it back to the bottom. When I fish herring, I fish with a big net. We catch around 20 000 pounds of herring every day that we have to shake out with our hands. It's a very messy job, and we get fish scales all over our faces!

Do you see seals when you are fishing? What do they remind you of — Kyla
We do see many seals! In fact there is a rock near where I grew up that's called Seal Rock. I think seals have always reminded me of puppies... big fat puppies! Even the grown-up ones.

Have you ever seen a mermaid out there? — Trypp
Only in my dreams.

What is the scariest moment you've ever had fishing? — Ashley
Thankfully I haven't had many scary moments because I have always been careful and had very safe skippers [*bosses*]. However, once I fell overboard, and another time I was sleeping in my bunk and a wave came over the boat that was so big, water came in my room!

Have you always liked to fish? — Jodie
I didn't like it when I was a kid, but I had to help my father because it was part of my upbringing. It wasn't until I graduated from school and tried many different jobs that I realized fishing was something I loved. All of the old fisherman say "it's in your blood," which is a saying that basically means it's a part of you, and you're drawn to it.

Do you recommend fishing as a job? — Roy
For sure! I encourage anyone who has the opportunity to go out on a commercial fishing vessel to give it a try. That includes you, girls! Some people have the silly idea that fishing is something men do, but I know many women who fish! Fishing can be very rewarding, and it can be a lot of fun. It also teaches you how to work hard, be organized, think for yourself, and how to work closely with others. It may not be for everyone, but it's a great job if you like it.

For these students, the out-of-school interview reflected their lives, while for me it opened up a life that was very different from mine, and so worth learning about.

How do I handle issues of culture, gender, and diversity in literacy?

How important is a student's culture to literacy growth? Extremely important. Researchers have identified six knowledge bases needed for teaching in a diverse classroom: self-knowledge, linguistic knowledge, culturally informed knowledge, knowledge of multicultural materials, knowledge of literacy methods, and knowledge of home/school relationships. We need to integrate the home and school worlds of every student so that parents and caregivers can work alongside the school in supporting literacy for all children.

As teachers we want to examine the issues pertaining to the literacy lives of all boys and girls, how they perceive themselves as readers, and how parents, teachers, and peers influence their literacy development. A variety of texts gives us resources for meeting the needs of the students and the curriculum. We need to understand and appreciate the developing characteristics and behaviours of students in a variety of literacy situations, and recognize the effect of gender, culture, and social issues on their developing literacy lives. Helping and freeing students to respond honestly and without fear to texts by engaging in activities such as discussion groups, artistic interpretations, journal writing, and drama, enables individuals to find and share their own voices, to be accepted as equal members of the community called school.

Schools need to focus on issues of diversity in literacy, taking advantage of differences in age, gender, dialect, language, and culture, seeing them as advantages for interactive teaching. Emilia Ferreiro, an authority on the relationships between language and literacy, writes in her book *Past and Present of the Verbs to Read and to Write*, "We need to see the contexts for building community between and despite difference."

In a literature circle project exploring gender in the frame of shared novels, I was working with teachers and sixth-grade students in two different cities over three months. As a final meeting, we organized a teleconference between the two school districts during which students at each school could see and hear students at the other campus. Everyone had opportunities for joining the conversation and responding to the questions that were asked concerning their responses to the books they had read. Dianne Stevens, our researcher, then analyzed the journals and the conversations, and we found some differences that could be attributed to gender, but also many common responses. The following came from students in both schools about one of the novels we had discussed, *Egghead* by Caroline Pignat, and you can observe some of the issues of gender that concerned the students. Two of the main characters in the book, Will and Shane, are both in grade nine, and are caught up in the bullying of Will.

- Bullying actually exists (obviously) and happens in life.
- The bigger and stronger people go after the weak, nerdy, easy target, like Will.
- This story really connects to real life because in high school there is usually a bully and two or more friends to back him up.
- Shane's group is nothing like life. I don't think anyone would go that far in bullying.
- Many people stick up for others who are being bullied.
- We don't have bullies at our school, so I don't know how I would react to a bully.
- Girls get bullied as many times as boys do.

- If Katie were the one being bullied, being a girl, she would try to change and be less of a target.
- Boys would not involve a girl in their bully group.
- More boys bully boys. Girls bully girls about makeup and random things.
- If the female characters were males, the story would be more physical because more boys, more fighting.
- Girls and boys both stand up to bullying.
- I probably would stand up for myself more than Will did.
- I do stand up to bullying. Usually I'm the one getting bullied though.
- Adults like to know what is happening, except kids don't usually tell them.
- I think the teachers at my school would care more than Will's school did.
- All these people are different types that are in real life, such as the bully (Shane), the bullied (Will) and the guy that's stuck in the middle (Devan).
- Some girls, like Katie, are understanding and feel sorry for geeks who are being bullied.
- I find usually bullies taunt their own gender.
- Most girls don't get bullied as much as boys.
- I've been like all of them at one point: I've been bullied, I have bullied and I've just stood by.
- We can find so much learning inside these statements for us as teachers, when we take time to read as authentic readers. During the book discussions with the students over several months, many of these concerns were voiced, and their journals opened the issues even further. The final two-city sharing brought other facets of the issues to the students' understandings. Novels are powerful emotional agents; they drive student responses into deep, deep water, within the safe frame of fiction.

How do I help ESL learners achieve success in my reading/writing programs?

Many years ago I was working with Inuit students in Sanikiluaq, a municipality and Inuit community located on the north coast of Flaherty Island in Hudson Bay. I felt utterly inadequate because of my lack of knowledge about their culture and language, but they were generous and accommodating and I survived the two-week session. As I was leaving to board the plane home, an Inuit boy handed me a poem he had written. He said it was the only poem he had ever written, and he wanted me to have it. I was a stranger, a safe reader for his secret poem, and I have kept it for thirty years.

> Musk Ox:
> Hey Goose, can you find my wife?
> I really need my wife. Do you know where my wife is?
> If you tell me where my wife is, I will save you from the hunter.
> I am suffering for my wife.
> Sea Gull:
> You'll never know where your wife is.
> I married her yesterday.
> She said she loved me.
>
> — Johnny

Such a haunting poem, filled with cultural knowledge, folklore, yearning, sadness, and written for me in English. How strange that the form of communication we seldom turn to as adults seems for many young people the most accessible means of voicing very deep feelings and perceptions. I value this boy's life, his world, his words in our shared language.

Schools today reflect the growing diversity of our population. Increasingly, especially within large urban centres, there are large numbers of students who are new to the area, or to the country, and inexperienced with the English language. At the same time, there are pressures and expectations for schools to ensure that all students are developing their literacy skills and becoming effective English-language communicators. As a result, teachers are increasingly called on to provide specific supports to develop their students' literacy skills.

We need to be aware of some of our subjective assumptions about language and literacy — what we know as English may not be English at all to a child for whom English is a second language (ESL) or dialect (ESD). Even within what we call "Standard" English, society's many groups develop special words to communicate common interests, such as the jargon used by engineers, sports fans, and even teachers; and different generations use words and idioms in diverse ways. Many students come from homes where the language of the classroom is not spoken, either in the vocabulary used or the style chosen. Yet the need to communicate is common to all.

Some of these readers may face a special challenge. They are learning to read and write in English as a second language, but may already be literate in their home language. Although they share their peers' reading tastes, their level of English precludes them from reading many age-appropriate texts. These students generally do not want to read books that are read by younger students. High-interest, low-vocabulary novels were developed to fill this gap, but did not prove to be a great success because of their general lack of plot and character sophistication. But now we can find texts for these students that will appeal to their humour, their sense of adventure, and their need for a good story. Giving these students texts that are accessible and worth reading, and then structuring learning so that they can receive assistance and support as they read, will enable them to sustain their interest while advancing their literacy skills.

Teachers' expectations of and relationships with indigenous students — First Nations, Métis, and Inuit — profoundly affect their learning. Numerous research studies in literacy have shown that these students are more academically successful when they feel welcomed, valued, and challenged by material that builds upon their prior knowledge, experiences, and interests. When these attitudes, behaviours, and curriculum considerations are missing, students from culturally and linguistically diverse backgrounds may miss out on school. We need to celebrate the lives of all our students, and to do that sometimes we teachers must be quiet and listen while they do the talking.

Jim Cummins is a recognized authority on ESL and ELL education, and his book with Margaret Early, *Big Ideas for Expanding Minds*, is a welcome support for teachers.

How do I help students with special requirements in a regular classroom?

We have to offer enough supportive strategies to a child in difficulty to ensure a successful school life. It may be that some students will need other environments, other structures, in order to progress. But to paraphrase the psychoanalyst D. W. Winnicott, we have to be "the good enough teacher," and for me therein lies the struggle. I need to know that I did all that I could at that time in those circumstances, with that particular child. By remembering my own experiences with students at risk, I look at every new child differently. I have the opportunity to grow wiser because of that special child. The "felt imperative" to help every child in our care is good for every teacher to experience. Perhaps, though, it has to be tempered with our professional sense of having done everything we could at that time for that child, strengthened by the knowledge that the experience of knowing these students and their parents will nudge us towards new understandings in our relationships with others in the place called school.

My colleague Shelley Murphy teaches and writes on this issue, and has wiser words than mine:

> Some students have more difficulty than others in their literacy learning. Whether students are striving learners or have a documented special education need, many of the considerations are the same. Students need:
> - differentiated instruction that responds to their individual needs. Teachers begin by determining a starting point for their students' learning. They do by gaining a better understanding of student's strengths and challenges, readiness to learn, interests, and learning styles through formal and informal assessment such as learning style inventories, teacher-student conferencing, observations, miscue analysis etc.
> - to be taught strategies, explicitly. Teachers instruct explicitly by sharing the purpose for learning a new skill with their students, by giving clear explanations and demonstrations of what students will learn, and by providing ongoing, supported practice with feedback until students become independent.
> - to be grouped, flexibly. Teachers purposely and strategically group and regroup students in a variety of ways throughout the school day so they are more easily able to address learners' specific needs. Students may be grouped according to their interests, reading/writing ability, learning style, language proficiency etc. Students have the opportunity to work with, and learn from, their peers while being supported by the teacher.
> - choice. When students are offered choice, it provides them with a sense of control, purpose, and competence which helps to improve motivation and engagement. For example, teachers can offer choice in learning activities, content, timelines, with whom and where students will complete their work, and how they will demonstrate their understanding etc.
> - ongoing opportunities for success. When students have regular opportunities to succeed in their literacy experiences, they are more likely to voluntarily engage in literacy activities and take the risks they need to become more proficient and independent learners.

Some students may need specialized equipment such as braillers, magnification aids, word processors with spell checkers, and other computer programs with peripherals such as voice synthesizers or large print to help achieve outcomes. Speaking and listening outcomes can be understood to include all forms of verbal and non-verbal communication, including sign language and communicators.

The Language Arts Curriculum. Departments of Education of New Brunswick, Newfoundland and Labrador, Nova Scotia, and Prince Edward Island

7

How can I use tests to teach?

How do I know how my students are doing?
What do I do next?

As caring teachers, we want to develop assessment strategies and use evaluation to help our students recognize their strengths and recognize their weaknesses. Then we can design useful instruction for supporting their literacy growth.

Assessment (what we discover to direct our teaching) and evaluation (how we measure and report a student's proficiency) are essential components of our teaching plans, and we can implement assessment strategies every day. We need to determine what a student or group of students know, how they learn best, and their capabilities and needs, as we observe their literacy behaviours and competencies, so that we can develop and modify our programs to be as effective as possible. We can use a broad variety of indicators that track our students' progress and achievements.

Assessment is an ongoing process of gathering and recording information about students' learning through anecdotal records, inventories, surveys, checklists, observations, portfolios, writing folders, conferencing, running records, audio and video recording, and student self-assessment. Summative assessment and evaluation occur at the end of the unit or year, and involve conferring, analysis, grading, and reporting. Results can also serve as feedback for modifying our subsequent literacy programs.

We can assess student growth consistently as part of the regular classroom program whenever possible by listening to the child read aloud in a conference, or by conducting a running record. Within demonstrations and mini-lessons, we can often orally direct students to respond to test-like questions in a situation where the pressure to be correct is less daunting than in a testing situation. These little practice sessions can help prepare them for formal testing events. After a test, it is useful to stress what the child knew and understood, to build on positive aspects of the experience, and to then move into remedial work.

Our goal of assessment that teaches rather than just rewarding or punishing was brought home to me a few years ago when a poem I had written was part of a provincial literacy test. One teacher copied some of his students' responses and sent them to me. Their work gave me great hope; even on a test, they were able to find their voices and carve out anecdotes to support their reading. This was an example of assessment and evaluation working as a team. We can test and still teach. Here is my poem, followed by sample student responses:

HERE WE GO LOBSTER LOO

I went to a very expensive restaurant
With my Aunt (in Halifax).
She said to have lobster,
Melt-in-the-mouth lobster,
But she didn't tell me
The lobster's alive,
All red and crawling
In an old aquarium.
I chose the saddest one.
They boiled him alive.
Alive.

I listened to my plate.
No sound.
Then I took pliers
And cracked and crushed
And scraped the pink flesh
Into my red mouth.
I told her I loved lobster.
(But they belong in
Nova Scotia
With my grandfather,
Not on my fork.)

Student responses:

I chose to write about this poem because it reminds me of myself when my father brought Lobster home to be prepared for dinner. I did not know Lobsters were to be alive before cooking. Looking at those poor innocent creatures being prepared to go into the pot of boiling death water made me cry because they were alive when father brought them home, but with no sound or movement on my plate.

The part of the poem which mentions "The expensive restaurant" did the same to me as it did to the Boy because I had to eat it, very upsetting to me but I had to eat it. Many of my family members did. I did not want to see my father upset because of the tremendous effort needed to catch these creatures and for me not to eat them would break my father's heart.

To devour them like that made me cry not physically, but mentally. For, in my mind I also heard screaming. Horrifying screams coming from my lobster as I cracked him, crushed him, scraped flesh from his broken body and eat that flesh from the creature screaming, the screaming only heard by my ears.

In my mouth, the flesh from the creature tore at my glands, my taste buds and at my mind. The taste of this creature made me feel like spitting out, but the thoughts of my father's work catching the creatures made me eat.
I chew because there are many lobsters in the sea which I can make happy by letting them live among themselves but one father to make happy, by being his wonderful son.

How can I help students monitor their own reading progress?

I developed this reflective student questionnaire with a group of teachers who wanted their students in the middle years to think about their reading and responding progress. I suggested that the students select a text each month and think back to that particular reading experience. Their responses can offer us insights into how they see themselves as readers and constructors of knowledge, and perhaps give them a metacognitive look at their own processing strategies.

Reading Profile of a Text Experience

What did you read? (screen) (page)

Was there any assistance? (audio, etc.)

Who selected the text? (teacher) (government) (Internet) (you) (classmate)

Did you bring any background from your own life?

Would you have liked more background?

Did you predict what the text might be about?

What genre was the text? (narrative) (opinion) (information) (poem) (script) (test) (game) (report) (correspondence) (hybrid)

What mode was the text? (print) (speech) (visual) (sound) (combination)

Did you silently read/view the text? (alone) (group) (class)

Was the print text read aloud?

Was the reading/viewing interrupted with questions or discussion?

Did you have any difficulties while reading/viewing?

Were the sentences too complex?

Were some words technical or unfamiliar?

Was the text too long? Too short?

Was it too loaded with information?

Was the format unhelpful or complicated?

How did you handle any difficulties while reading/viewing? Did you:
- reread part or all of the text?
- seek help from the teacher, a classmate, an online reference?
- jot down questions to answer later?
- stop reading?

How did you respond after reading/viewing the text? (talk) (write) (arts) (research)

Did you make any connections to other texts, to your own life, or to world concerns?

Was reading/viewing this text useful to you?

What puzzlements about the text remain?

Do you disagree with any of the ideas in this text?

Knowing that self-assessment will form a part of their overall assessment helps students develop a sense of ownership of their learning and know that they can shape the course of their learning. Their contributions in conferences, notebooks and journals, portfolios, and discussions are all part of the self-assessment process. Sharing in their assessment helps students to recognize what they know, what they need to know and ways in which they can learn. Students begin to see themselves as readers and writers, thinkers and meaning-makers.

How do I know if I have an effective literacy program in my classroom?

In addition to assessing and evaluating students, we also need to evaluate our teaching programs to ascertain whether they actually help our students meet the goals we set for them. In part, program evaluation arises from the progress students make. We need to be sure that what we do in class, from selecting texts through assessing a student's responses, is sound and valid, and contributes to our students' overall development.

All of us — students and teachers — need to consider our effectiveness, our progress, our sense of personal and professional satisfaction. We grow from considering our lives, reflecting on our changes, talking to others about our shared concerns, connecting other aspects of our lives to what is going on in our work and our learning. We can become what we dream we can become. I need my network of significant others to nudge and motivate and support me, so that I will look up to discover the lake on the horizon and the satisfaction of my own growth.

The following questionnaire may serve as a starting point for your own reflective look at your classroom literacy program. These points depend on so many factors, and you need to clarify the context for your own particular assessment of the different aspects of teaching and learning. There will be times when timetabling is out of your control, when school programs intervene, when testing dominates the schedule. What I hope these questions will do is help you step back, look carefully, think about and rethink those parts of your program that could be strengthened, developed, and augmented with different resources.

You might want to create a student questionnaire to see literacy learning from their viewpoints. We are fortunate to be in a profession that allows us to work toward more effective strategies and techniques for supporting literacy growth with our students. I wish I could meet my former elementary students and start again with what we now have learned. But since I can't, I trust you to move everyone you teach onward as literate citizens.

- Is there a culture of literacy developing in your classroom, with a predictable and supportive schedule conducive to having students work together as a community, in small groups, and independently?
- What texts do you use for modeling your own literacy life?
- What types of texts do you use for read-alouds and think-alouds?
- Are your demonstrations helpful in showing students how effective readers and writers function?
- How do you organize the students for literacy activities in groups?
- When do you bring the classroom community together?
- What texts (in print and online) do you provide for independent reading?
- How do you find time to work with readers and writers in difficulty?
- Which response modes work best for your students? Which new ones could you try?
- Are there opportunities for writing and revising in a variety of modes and forms?
- How are you building language muscles with your students, so that they have the word and sentence power necessary for effective reading and writing?
- What ways have you found to provide differentiated literacy opportunities?
- Is the inquiry process at the heart of your teaching/learning dynamic in other areas of the curriculum?
- Do your students have a sense of ownership and satisfaction with their literacy work?
- Do you incorporate the Internet and school and public libraries into your classroom program?

- Do you create opportunities for moving critical learning experiences into greater engagement with the outside community, as in interacting with parents/guardians, working with volunteers, inviting guests into the classroom, going on field trips, interviewing authorities, using technology, and taking part in social action programs?
- Do you share with your colleagues classroom anecdotes, professional books, journal articles, and reports that offer strategies and structures for helping students deepen their literacy experiences?

Conclusion: Putting it all together

A literacy unit based on the picture book *Sleeping Boy*

While working in a school for a week, I was invited to visit a combined grade one- and -two classroom and explore some literacy strategies that would involve memoir writing. I thought this would be a good opportunity to explore the multitexts involved in such a unit — the printed text by Sonia Craddock, the illustrations by Leonid Gore, the children's conversations, memoir writing, role play, and the experiential texts the children bring to the work. I visited the class during their shared reading time over three mornings, as the teacher created a unit from these texts. Since a memoir is usually a written memory, I wanted to tie it to the students' responses to a story that they could explore as participants. They would be able to create a description of an event from the story, written in the first person, and told from one person's point of view. When developed in role, a memoir offers a vehicle for students to enter the emotional life of the role they are or have been playing, a reflective opportunity for them to inhabit the situation that was the focus of the response experience. A memoir can be written and shared after the reading and the explorations, as students revisit the implications of the story.

First lesson:

The teacher read aloud the picture book. *Sleeping Boy* has a very complex text; it's a modern allegory in which Sonia Craddock uses the framework of "Sleeping Beauty" to tell the story of war, setting her narrative in Berlin. At the birthday party for Knabe Rosen, the dreaded Major Krieg arrives and predicts: "On your sixteenth birthday you will hear the drums drumming as the army marches by. Off to war you'll go — and you will not come home." But the boy's aunt, Tante Taube, gives the boy her blessing: "Instead of going off to war, Knabe Rosen will only sleep ... sleep through poverty and war, bad times and sadness, until peace comes to Berlin." When the family awakes, the war is over, and life continues.

Second lesson:

The teacher knew her class well, and the students had experienced a wide variety of shared texts. This book presented some difficulties for me as a visitor: the war concepts were very sophisticated, but the telling and the visuals were aimed right at children. They asked to see the pictures up close after the reading. I was holding the book for this part of the unit, and listening to their comments and questions about the text, both the print story and the illustrations. I was surprised at their knowledge of the construct of war. They seemed so young, but as they discussed issues that concerned them, they revealed the stories underpinning the book, and shared home anecdotes and family histories that deepened the narrative they had listened to.

Third lesson:

We began to imagine the characters referenced in the text, and the students took on roles and spoke as if they had experienced those lives But their true interests lay in the destructive nature of war, and the dialogue became very animated with their sense of unfairness of being victims in a situation they had no control over.

Their responses to the story and the pictures brought out their questions about the war and the villages, both bombed and safe, and they then wrote in role as storytellers, offering their accounts and embedding their feelings in their fictional memoirs.

First-person storytelling:

My villig sleept though the war. It was a mirigel rilly. If your villig got bomd i'm rilly very soory.

Jessa

My story is that one day I was lisanin to the radeo when I hrad a spashl brodcast war mite be starting! We proparerda for the war. I was waching out the windo I saw the bouts and planes comeing! Owe arme ran to defand our tane.

Andrew

There was a Granny who blessed a wish that the child would sleep through war and her wish got mixed up and the holl village fell asleep for 5 years and all the other villages got blown up even my best friend brad maurice got blown up.

Geordie

My town got bomed and lots of people got shot. But i herd about a nother town where every body slept and when they woke up they wer un harmed it's wherede I just don't get it. How could they sleep for five years and not change age it's really wherde. One of my familly members had to go to the hospital to get surgerey.

Adrienne

How come your toen didet get bomed and our town did. Are forest got bomed and our hoses and apartment's are people got shot and yor's didet. I'm glad for yow.

Brendan

My villig as bommd. The other villig was not bommd and the other villig slept theroo a war. are villig is vary damiged.

Meredith

My teaching thoughts:

In their brief but heartfelt memoirs, you can observe how the first-person voice allows them to describe, recount, and comment on their perceptions of the story. The details of the story are clear in their brief retellings, and some personalize their memoirs with deep sadness or identify with the villagers who were victims of war. Their writings were first drafts since we wanted their immediate responses to the heart of the allegory, but their invented spellings did not hold them back from using significant words and terms to portray their thoughts. Dramatic voice frees students from the constraints of many writing tasks and supports the freedom to draw upon authentic thoughts and feelings. Each teacher will want to personalize approaches and activities according to the interests and abilities of their students, but this class demonstrates the inside/outside connections to a shared text, moving from general statements about the effects of battle ("are villig is vary damaged") to the unjust pain caused to civilians ("How come your toen didet get bomed and our town did. Are forest got bomed and our hoses and apartment's are people got shot and yor's didet"), to the personal connections that they wove into the plot ("even my best friend brad maurice got blown up".) Their responses reveal a strong understanding of the text, of the far-reaching global effects of conflict, and the internalizing of the information into a personal recognition. This must be what comprehension means in our literacy lexicon. And I should point out the metacognitive response to text as a student questions the whole premise of the book: "it's wherede I just don't get it. How could they sleep for five years and not change age it's really wherde."

The students' abilities with written language are strong; there are no hesitations in their use of the words and structures they need to express their thoughts. The phonetic understanding of the spelling of "toen", where each pronounced syllable of "town" is heard and encoded, where "villig" is spelled as the word is heard, and "arme" has a vocalized "e". So much word knowledge to work with, to explore and extend. They will move into standardized spelling quickly and easily.

This unit involved the teacher's reading aloud of a shared and complicated text, with analogies and facts interwoven. The text talk was authentic and revealing, and led to the writing of memoirs with voices represented in role. The children's connections to self, text, and world are clear and powerful. We should celebrate the teacher and her students, and value the literacy processes involved in the different aspects of the work. How they understand the concerns of war as reflected in this multileveled picture book indicates the effect of culture — home and school and media — on their life constructs, and enlightens us to the impact of the multiple texts influencing their lives. We must not be afraid of what students have experienced; rather, we give them strategies for interpreting, interrogating, and reflecting upon the texts they encounter. We offer them safe venues for exploring the texts of their dreams and nightmares.

Given the same book with a different group of students, another teacher might have developed a different unit, emphasizing visual interpretations, or class re-enactment. Putting it all together means working with what seems best with these students at this time with this text.

This summer I will be teaching a graduate course in literacy education. I have planned the syllabus, selecting research articles and texts written by teachers who have articulated their classroom practice, and I will follow the processes I have outlined in this book for the reading/writing workshops: I want to present a PowerPoint talk on one aspect of the literacy program; the students will move into grade groupings and discuss the text assigned the day before, chosen to highlight the focused concern; we will share wise moments from the group talk, and record on the class website the main points; one group will present a YouTube video or film they have discovered about the issue, and we will have a general sharing about the comments and questions initiated by the work. Students will post online other responses to the class, and some dialogue will occur. We will use the questions suggested by the graduate students in this book as entry points to the learning events, and new queries will emerge, and students will begin creating their own versions of this book with extended insights and concerns about the teaching of literacy in our classrooms. Learning is fluid and continuing; each attempt at an answer is simply a marker on the literacy journey.

I will want to hear my graduate students' own literacy-life stories, of their first experiences with printed texts, their school events that remained memorable (for good or for difficult reasons), their choices of texts they want to or have to read now (the ones they appreciate, the ones that cause pain). I will want them to learn from each other, to be excited by a research article we find that strengthens their understanding, to meet a teacher/author who articulates in her book a passion for teaching well, to discover a picture book that demands being shared with a class, a biography that awakens children to the power of writing, online images and graphics that speak volumes — all this in a summer course. But like all teachers, I dream large, and that is the joy of working with students of all ages. And I hope their culminating papers will represent their own interests, not mine, and that I will find their sense-making about literacy behaviours and events honest, referenced by the work of others in the field, and well-crafted with professionalism but also marked by their own unfolding journeys.

All of us will have to follow the trail of breadcrumbs back through the forest to childhood, where students truly live, so that we can remember who we were, once upon a time, entering school, letting go of our parents' hands, and joining the world of literacy.

Clare Kosnik, Jennifer Rowsell, and Peter Williamson have collected a series of articles by international educators in *Literacy Teacher Educators: Preparing Teachers for a Changing World*, which examines the roles of those working in teacher education, and considers the impact of their programs on those young people who will teach literacy in the continually changing world of learning.

Acknowledgments

I want to thank the research team who helped me develop this book. Larry Swartz and the teacher candidates in his literacy class offered their core questions about the practice of teaching literacy, and these formed the basis for this book.

My colleague Richard Coles is a stalwart teacher/researcher, and he provided me with new studies and articles from his constant quest for thoughtful research and practice in the teaching of literacy. All teachers need a Richard Coles to keep them growing and honest.

My colleague Shelley Stagg Peterson shared the large compendiums of research journals published by the International Literacy Association over the last two decades, and they became a rich source for our conversations, and for strengthening my *theory into practice* approach to answering questions about literacy.

The helpful books I have listed alongside my answers are from the shelves in my office, and their authors are practitioners who believe strongly in researched classroom practice. They offer teachers thoughtful ways to promote learning/teaching events that can change the lives of our students forever.

Bibliography

Allen, Janet. *Yellow Brick Roads: Shared and Guided Paths to Independent Reading 4–12*. Stenhouse, 2000.

Alvermann, Donna, Norman Unrau, and Robert Ruddell. *Theoretical Models and Processes of Reading*. International Reading Association, 2013.

Atwell, Nancie. *In the Middle*. Heinemann, 1998.

Barrs, Myra, Robert Barton, and David Booth. *This Book Is Not About Drama: It's About New Ways to Inspire Students*. Pembroke, 2012.

Barton, Bob. *Telling Stories Your Way: Storytelling and Reading Aloud in the Classroom*. Pembroke, 2000.

Baskwill, Jane. *Attention-Grabbing Tools for Involving Parents in Their Children's Learning*. Pembroke, 2013.

Benevides, Tina. "How Guided Dialogue Encourages Rethinking." In *Exploding the Reading* by David Booth. Pembroke, 2014.

Bomer, Randy, and Katherine Bomer. *For a Better World: Reading and Writing for Social Action*, Heinemann, 2001.

Booth, David. *Caught in the Middle*. Pembroke, 2011.

Booth, David. *I've Got Something to Say!* Pembroke, 2013.

Booth, David. *It's Critical: Classroom Strategies for Promoting Critical and Creative Comprehension*. Pembroke, 2008.

Booth, David. *Whatever Happened to Language Arts?* Pembroke, 2009.

Booth, David, and Kathy Gould Lundy. *In Graphic Detail: Using Graphic Novels in the Classroom*. Rubicon, 2007.

Booth, David, and Larry Swartz. *Learning to Read with Graphic Power*. Rubicon, 2006.

Booth, David, and Larry Swartz. *Literacy Techniques*. Pembroke, 2004.

Burke, Anne. *Ready to Learn: Using Play to Build Literacy Skills in Young Learners*. Pembroke, 2010.

Clay, Marie M. *An Observation Survey of Early Literacy Achievement*. Heinemann, 2006.

Cleary, Beverly. *Dear Mr. Henshaw*. HarperCollins, 2001.

Creech, Sharon. *Love That Dog*. HarperCollins, 2008.

Craddock, Sonia. *Sleeping Boy*. Atheneum, 1999.

Cummins, Jim, and Margaret Early. *Big Ideas for Expanding Minds*. Pearson Canada, 2014.

Cunningham, Katie Egan. *Story: Still the Heart of Literacy Learning*. Stenhouse, 2015.

Cunningham, Patricia. *Phonics They Use: Words for Reading and Writing* (6th edition). Pearson, 2012.

Daniels, Harvey, and Nancy Steineke. *Texts and Lessons for Content-Area Reading*. Heinemann, 2011.

Daniels, Harvey. *Literature Circles* (2nd edition). Stenhouse, 2002.

Demacio, Jeff. "How Engagement Leads to Inspiration and Passion for Learning." In *Caught in the Middle* by David Booth. Pembroke, 2011.

Dietze, Beverlie, and Diane Kashin. *Playing and Learning in Early Childhood*. Pearson Canada, 2012.

Diller, Debbie. *Literacy Work Stations*. Stenhouse, 2003.

Donohue. Lisa. *Independent Reading Inside the Box*. Pembroke, 2008.

Dorfman, Lynne, and Diane Dougherty. *Grammar Matters*. Stenhouse, 2014.

Eeds, Maryann, and Ralph Peterson. *Grand Conversations*. Scholastic, 2007.

Egan, Kieran. *An imaginative Approach to Teaching*. John Wiley and Sons, 2005.

Farstrup, Allan, and S. Jay Samuals, eds. *What Research Has to Say About Reading Instruction*. International Reading Association, 2002.

Ferreiro, Emilia. *Past and Present of the Verbs to Read and to Write*. Groundwood, 2003.

Follett, Corey. "Building a Unit on Afghanistan with Multitexts." In *It's Critical!* by David Booth, Pembroke, 2008.

Fountas, Irene, and Gay Su Pinnell. *Guiding Readers and Writers*. Heinemann, 2000.

Freire, Paulo. *Pedagogy of Freedom*. Rowman and Littlefield, 1998.

Fullan, Michael. *Stratosphere: Integrating Technology, Pedagogy, and Change Knowledge*. Pearson Canada, 2013.

Gallagher, Kelly. *In the Best Interest of Students: Staying True to What Works in the ELA Classroom*. Stenhouse, 2015.

Gallas, Karen. *Imagination and Literacy*. Teachers College Press, 2003.

Gear, Adrienne. *Reading Power*. Pembroke, 2015.

Gee, James. *Literacy and Education*. Routledge: Key Ideas in Education, 2014.

Gerstein, Mordicai. *The Seal Mother*. Puffin, 1990.

Graves, Donald. *Writing: Teachers and Children at Work, 20th Anniversary Edition*. Heinemann, 2003.

Greene, Maxine. *Releasing the Imagination: Essays on Education, the Arts, and Social Change*. Jossey-Bass, 2000.

Harvey, Stephanie, and Anne Goudvis. *Strategies That Work*. Stenhouse, 2007.

Harvey, Stephanie, and Harvey "Smokey" Daniels. *Comprehension and Collaboration: Inquiry Circles for Curiosity, Engagement, and Understanding*. Heinemann, 2015.

Keene, Ellin Oliver, Susan Zimmermann, and Debbie Miller. *Comprehension: Going Forward*. Heinemann, 2011.

Klassen, Jon. *I Want My Hat Back*. Candlewick, 2011.

Kosnik, Clare, et al. *Building Bridges: Rethinking Literacy Teacher Education in a Digital Era*. Sense Publishers, 2016.

Kosnik, Clare, Jennifer Rowsell, and Peter Williamson, eds. *Literacy Teacher Educators: Preparing Teachers for a Changing World*. Sense Publishers, 2013.

Kress, Gunther. "Design and Transformation: New Theories of Meaning." In *Multiliteracies*, edited by Bill Cope and Mary Kalantzis. Routledge, 2000.

Layne, Steven. *In Defense of Read-Aloud*. Stenhouse, 2015.

Lee, Royan. "Sharing Thoughts through Blogging." In *Caught in the Middle* by David Booth. Pembroke, 2011.

Luke, Allan, and Peter Freebody. "A Map of Possible Practices." In *Four Resources Model*. Practically Primary, 4, 5–8. 1999.

Lundy, Kathy Gould. *Conquering the Crowded Curriculum*. Pembroke, 2016.

Marshall, James. "George and Martha" Complete Series. HMH Books for Young Readers, 2006.

Martin, Bill, Jr. *Brown Bear, Brown Bear*. Henry Holt, 1967.

McCallum, Deborah. *The Feedback Friendly Classroom*. Pembroke, 2015.

Mills, David. "Promoting Literacy in Visual Arts: Banners on a Social Justice Theme." In *Caught in the Middle* by David Booth. Pembroke, 2011.

Oppel, Kenneth. *Silverwing*. HarperCollins, 1997.

Overmeyer, Mark. *Let's Talk: One-on-One, Peer and Small Group Conferences*. Pembroke, 2015.

Overturf, Brenda, Leslie Montgomery, and Margot Holmes-Smith. *Word Nerds: Teaching All Students to Love Vocabulary*. Stenhouse, 2013.

Peterson, Shelley Stagg. "How Am I Doing? Feedback for Improving Student Writing." In *Caught in the Middle* by David Booth. Pembroke, 2011.

Peterson, Shelley Stagg. *Writing Across the Curriculum: All Teachers Teach Writing.* Portage and Main, 2008.

Peterson, Shelley Stagg, and David Booth. *Why Leveled Books Have a Specific and Limited Role in Teaching Reading. https://www.oise.utoronto.ca/cerll/ UserFiles/File/Resources/LeveledBooks_StaggPeterson_Booth.pdf*

Pignat, Caroline. *Egghead.* Red Deer Press, 2007.

Pinnell, Gay Su, and Irene Fountas. *When Readers Struggle.* Heinemann, 2009.

Reasoner, Charles F. *Releasing Children to Literature.* Dell, 1976.

REEL CANADA: Dedicated to bringing Canadian films to students. Email contactus@reelcanada.ca to get started. Or by phone 416.642.5796. Toll-free 1.855.733.5709. Fax 647.557.2111

Robinson, Amy, and Lauren Miller. "Reading Rocks: A Reading Mentoring Program." In *Caught in the Middle* by David Booth. Pembroke, 2011.

Rog, Lori Jamison. *Guiding Readers.* Pembroke, 2012.

Rosen, Betty. *And None of It Was Nonsense: The Power of Storytelling in School.* Scholastic, 1988.

Rowsell, Jennifer. *Working with Multimodality.* Routledge, 2013.

Satrapi, Marjane. *Persepolis*, Books 1 and 2. Pantheon, 2003.

Scott-Dunne, Doreen. *When Spelling Matters.* Pembroke, 2013.

Sebastian, Kevin. "Achieving Student Engagement by Seeking Social Justice." In *Caught in the Middle* by David Booth. Pembroke, 2011.

Serafini, Frank. *Reading the Visual: An Introduction to Teaching Multimodal Literacy.* Teachers College, Columbia University, 2013.

Sewell, Anna. *Black Beauty.* Puffin, 2008.

Styles, Donna. *Class Meetings.* Pembroke, 2001.

Swartz, Larry, and Shelley Stagg Peterson. *This Is a Great Book.* Pembroke, 2015.

Tompkins, Gail. *50 Literacy Strategies.* Pearson, 2013.

Tovani, Cris. *I Read It But I Don't Get It.* Stenhouse, 2000.

Wilhelm, Jeff, Erika Boas, and Peggy Jo Wilhelm. *Inquiring Minds: Learn to Read and Write.* Scholastic, 2007.

Wilson, Donna, and Marcus Conyers. www.brainsmart.org

Winnicott, D. W. *Playing and Reality.* Routledge, 2005.

Yee, Paul. *Tales from Gold Mountain.* Groundwood, 2011.

Yolen, Jane. *Encounter.* HMH Books for Young Readers, 1996.

Yolen, Jane. "The Promise." In *Here There Be Unicorns.* Harcourt, 1994.

Index